# ZEN
# FLESH
# ZEN
# BONES

# ZEN
# FLESH

A COLLECTION OF ZEN

# ZEN

AND PRE-ZEN WRITINGS

# BONES

禪骨
肉禪

*Compiled by Paul Reps and Nyogen Senzaki*

TUTTLE PUBLISHING
Tokyo • Rutland, Vermont • Singapore

Published by Tuttle Publishing, an imprint of Periplus Editions (HK)
Ltd., with editorial offices at 364 Innovation Drive, North Clarendon,
Vermont 05759 U.S.A.

Library of Congress Control Number: 57010199

ISBN 978-0-8048-3706-4

**Distributed by:**

**North America, Latin America and Europe**
Tuttle Publishing
364 Innovation Drive, North Clarendon, VT 05759-9436
Tel: 1 (802) 773-8930   Fax: 1 (802) 773-6993
Email: info@tuttlepublishing.com
Web site: www.tuttlepublishing.com

**Japan**
Tuttle Publishing
Yaekari Building, 3F, 5-4-12 Osaki, Shinagawa-ku. Tokyo 141-0032
Tel: (81) 3 5437 0171   Fax: (81) 3 5437 0755
Email: tuttle-sales@gol.com

**Asia Pacific**
Berkeley Books Pte. Ltd.
61 Tai Seng Avenue #02-12, Singapore 534167
Tel: (65) 6280-1330   Fax: (65) 6280-6290
inquiries@periplus.com.sg
www.periplus.com

12 11 10 09 08   10 9 8 7 6 5 4 3 2 1

Printed in Singapore

# Contents

THE GATELESS GATE

    BY EKAI, CALLED MU-MON TRANSCRIBED

    BY NYOGEN SENZAKI AND PAUL REPS ........*119*

# Foreword

THIS book includes four books:

*101 Zen Stories* was first published in 1939 by Rider and Company, London, and David McKay Company, Philadelphia. These stories recount actual experiences of Chinese and Japanese Zen teachers over a period of more than five centuries.

*The Gateless Gate* was first published in 1934 by John Murray, Los Angeles. It is a collection of problems called koan that Zen teachers use in guiding their students toward release, first recorded by a Chinese master in the year 1228.

*10 Bulls* was first published in 1935 by DeVorss and Company, Los Angeles, and subsequently by Ralph R. Phillips, Portland, Oregon. It is a translation from the Chinese of a famous twelfth-century commentary upon the stages of awareness leading to enlightenment and is here illustrated by one of Japan's best contemporary woodblock artists.

*Centering*, a transcription of ancient Sanskrit manuscripts, first appeared in the Spring 1955 issue of *Gentry* magazine, New York. It presents an ancient teaching, still alive in Kashmir and parts of India after more than four thousand years, that may well be the roots of Zen.

Thanks are due the publishers named above for permission to gather the material together here. And most of all am I grateful to Nyogen Senzaki, "homeless monk," exemplar-friend-collaborator, who so delighted with me in transcribing the first three books, even as that prescient man of Kashmir, Lakshmanjoo, did on the fourth.

The first Zen patriarch, Bodhidharma, brought Zen to China from India in the sixth century. According to his biography recorded in the year 1004 by the Chinese teacher Dogen, after nine years in China Bodhidharma wished to go home and gathered his disciples about him to test their apperception.

Dofuku said: "In my opinion, truth is beyond affirmation or negation, for this is the way it moves."

Bodhidharma replied: "You have my skin." The nun Soji said: "In my view, it is like Ananda's sight of the Buddha-land—seen once and forever."

Bodhidharma answered: "You have my flesh." Doiku said: "The four elements of light, airiness, fluidity, and solidity are empty (i.e., inclusive) and the five skandhas are no-things. In my opinion, no-thing (i.e., spirit) is reality."

Bodhidharma commented: "You have my bones."

Finally, Eka bowed before the master—and remained silent.

Bodhidharma said: "You have my marrow."

Old Zen was so fresh it became treasured and remembered. Here are fragments of its skin, flesh, bones, but not its marrow—never found in words.

The directness of Zen has led many to believe it stemmed from sources before the time of Buddha, 500 B.C. The reader may judge for himself, for he has here for the first time in one book the experiences of Zen, the mind problems, the stages of awareness, and a similar teaching predating Zen by centuries.

The problem of our mind, relating conscious to preconscious awareness, takes us deep into everyday living. Dare we open our doors to the source of our being? What are flesh and bones for?

—Paul Reps

# 101 ZEN STORIES

*Transcribed by Nyogen Senzaki and Paul Reps*

THESE stories were transcribed into English from a book called the Shaseki-shu (Collection of Stone and Sand), written late in the thirteenth century by the Japanese Zen teacher Muju (the "non-dweller"), and from anecdotes of Zen monks taken from various books published in Japan around the turn of the present century.

For Orientals, more interested in being than in busyness, the self-discovered man has been the most worthy of respect. Such a man proposes to open his consciousness just as the Buddha did.

These are stories about such self-discoveries.

The following is adapted from the preface to the first edition of these stories in English.

Zen might be called the inner art and design of the Orient. It was rooted in China by Bodhidharma, who came from India in the sixth century, and was carried eastward into Japan by the twelfth century. It has been described as: "A special teaching without scriptures, beyond words and letters, pointing to the mind-essence of man, seeing directly into one's nature, attaining enlightenment."

*Zen was known as Ch'an in China. The Ch'an-Zen mas-ters, instead of being followers of the Buddha, aspire to be his friends and to place themselves in the same responsive relationship with the universe as did Buddha and Jesus. Zen is not a sect but an experience.*

*The Zen habit of self-searching through meditation to realize one's true nature, with disregard of formalism, with insistence on self-discipline and simplicity of living, ulti-mately won the support of the nobility and ruling classes in Japan and the profound respect of all levels of philosophical thought in the Orient.*

*The Noh dramas are Zen stories. Zen spirit has come to mean not only peace and understanding, but devotion to art and to work, the rich unfoldment of contentment, opening the door to insight, the expression of innate beauty, the in-tangible charm of incompleteness. Zen carries many mean-ings, none of them entirely definable. If they are defined, they are not Zen.*

*It has been said that if you have Zen in your life, you have no fear, no doubt, no unnecessary craving, no extreme emotion. Neither illiberal attitudes nor egotistical actions trouble you. You serve humanity humbly, fulfilling your presence in this world with loving-kindness and observing your passing as a petal falling from a flower. Serene, you enjoy life in blissful tranquility. Such is the spirit of Zen, whose vesture is thousands of temples in China and Japan, priests and monks, wealth and prestige, and often the very formalism it would itself transcend.*

*To study Zen, the flowering of one's nature, is no easy task in any age or civilization. Many teachers, true and false, have purposed to assist others in this accomplishment. It is from innumerable and actual adventures in Zen that these stories have evolved. May the reader in turn realize them in living experience today.*

空 *1. A Cup of Tea*

NAN-IN, a Japanese master during the Meiji era (1868-1912), received a university professor who came to inquire about Zen.

Nan-in served tea. He poured his visitor's cup full, and then kept on pouring.

The professor watched the overflow until he no longer could restrain himself. "It is overfull. No more will go in!"

"Like this cup," Nan-in said, "you are full of your own opinions and speculations. How can I show you Zen unless you first empty your cup?"

不
歸 *2. Finding a Diamond
on a Muddy Road*

GUDO WAS the emperor's teacher of his time. Nevertheless, he used to travel alone as a wandering mendicant. Once when he was on his way to Edo, the cultural and political center of the shogunate, he approached a little village named Takenaka. It was evening and a heavy rain was falling. Gudo was thoroughly wet. His straw sandals were in pieces. At a farmhouse near the village he noticed four or five pairs of sandals in the window and decided to buy some dry ones.

The woman who offered him the sandals, seeing how wet he was, invited him to remain for the night in her home. Gudo accepted, thanking her. He entered and recited a sutra before the family shrine. He then was introduced to the woman's mother, and to her children. Observing that the entire family was depressed, Gudo asked what was wrong.

"My husband is a gambler and a drunkard," the housewife told him. "When he happens to win he drinks and becomes abusive. When he loses he borrows money from others. Sometimes when he becomes thoroughly drunk he does not come home at all. What can I do?"

"I will help him," said Gudo. "Here is some money. Get me a gallon of fine wine and something good to eat. Then you may retire. I will meditate before the shrine."

When the man of the house returned about midnight, quite drunk, he bellowed: "Hey, wife, I am home. Have you something for me to eat?"

"I have something for you," said Gudo. "I happened to be caught in the rain and your wife kindly asked me to remain here for the night. In return I have bought some wine and fish, so you might as well have them."

The man was delighted. He drank the wine at once and laid himself down on the floor. Gudo sat in meditation beside him.

In the morning when the husband awoke he had forgotten about the previous night. "Who are you? Where do you come from?" he asked Gudo, who still was meditating.

"I am Gudo of Kyoto and I am going on to Edo," replied the Zen master.

The man was utterly ashamed. He apologized profusely to the teacher of his emperor.

Gudo smiled. "Everything in this life is impermanent," he explained. "Life is very brief. If you keep on gambling and drinking, you will have no time left to accomplish anything else, and you will cause your family to suffer too."

The perception of the husband awoke as if from a dream. "You are right," he declared. "How can I ever repay you for this wonderful teaching! Let me see you off and carry your things a little way."

"If you wish," assented Gudo.

The two started out. After they had gone three miles Gudo told him to return. "Just another five miles," he begged Gudo. They continued on.

"You may return now," suggested Gudo.

"After another ten miles," the man replied.

"Return now," said Gudo, when the ten miles had been passed.

"I am going to follow you all the rest of my life," declared the man.

Modern Zen teachers in Japan spring from the lineage of a famous master who was the successor of Gudo. His name was Mu-nan, the man who never turned back.

# 斯 3. *Is That So?*

THE ZEN MASTER Hakuin was praised by his neighbors as one living a pure life.

A beautiful Japanese girl whose parents owned a food store lived near him. Suddenly, without any warning, her parents discovered she was with child. This made her parents angry. She would not confess who the man was, but after much harassment at last named Hakuin.

In great anger the parents went to the master. "Is that so?" was all he would say.

After the child was born it was brought to Hakuin. By this time he had lost his reputation, which did not trouble him, but he took very good care of the child. He obtained milk from his neighbors and everything else the little one needed.

A year later the girl-mother could stand it no longer. She told her parents the truth—that the real father of the child was a young man who worked in the fishmarket.

The mother and father of the girl at once went to Hakuin to ask his forgiveness, to apologize at length, and to get the child back again.

Hakuin was willing. In yielding the child, all he said was: "Is that so?"

# 尋 4. Obedience

THE MASTER Bankei's talks were attended not only by Zen students but by persons of all ranks and sects. He never quoted sutras nor indulged in scholastic dissertations. Instead, his words were spoken directly from his heart to the hearts of his listeners.

His large audiences angered a priest of the Nichiren sect because the adherents had left to hear about Zen. The self-centered Nichiren priest came to the temple, determined to debate with Bankei.

"Hey, Zen teacher!" he called out. "Wait a minute. Whoever respects you will obey what you say, but a man like myself does not respect you. Can you make me obey you?"

"Come up beside me and I will show you," said Bankei.

Proudly the priest pushed his way through the crowd to the teacher.

Bankei smiled. "Come over to my left side."

The priest obeyed.

"No," said Bankei, "we may talk better if you are on the right side. Step over here."

The priest proudly stepped over to the right.

"You see," observed Bankei, "you are obeying me and I think you are a very gentle person. Now sit down and listen."

## 愛 5. If You Love, Love Openly

TWENTY MONKS and one nun, who was named Eshun, were practicing meditation with a certain Zen master.

Eshun was very pretty even though her head was shaved and her dress plain. Several monks secretly fell in love with her. One of them wrote her a love letter, insisting upon a private meeting.

Eshun did not reply. The following day the master gave a lecture to the group, and when it was over, Eshun arose. Addressing the one who had written her, she said: "If you really love me so much, come and embrace me now."

情 *6. No Loving-Kindness*

THERE WAS an old woman in China who had supported a monk for over twenty years. She had built a little hut for him and fed him while he was meditating. Finally she wondered just what progress he had made in all this time.

To find out, she obtained the help of a girl rich in desire. "Go and embrace him," she told her, "and then ask him suddenly: 'What now?'"

The girl called upon the monk and without much ado caressed him, asking him what he was going to do about it.

"An old tree grows on a cold rock in winter," replied the monk somewhat poetically. "Nowhere is there any warmth."

The girl returned and related what he had said.

"To think I fed that fellow for twenty years!" exclaimed the old woman in anger. "He showed no consideration for your need, no disposition to explain your condition. He need not have responded to passion, but at least he should have evidenced some compassion."

She at once went to the hut of the monk and burned it down.

# 告 7. Announcement

TANZAN WROTE sixty postal cards on the last day of his life, and asked an attendant to mail them. Then he passed away.

The cards read:

> *I am departing from this world.*
> *This is my last announcement.*
> > *Tanzan.*
> > *July 27, 1892.*

# 浪 8. Great Waves

IN THE EARLY days of the Meiji era there lived a well-known wrestler called O-nami, Great Waves.

O-nami was immensely strong and knew the art of wrestling. In his private bouts he defeated even his teacher, but in public he was so bashful that his own pupils threw him.

O-nami felt he should go to a Zen master for help. Hakuju, a wandering teacher, was stopping in a little temple nearby, so O-nami went to see him and told him of his trouble.

"Great Waves is your name," the teacher advised, "so stay in this temple tonight. Imagine that you are those billows. You are no longer a wrestler who is afraid. You are those huge waves sweeping everything before them, swallowing all in their path. Do this and you will be the greatest wrestler in the land."

The teacher retired. O-nami sat in meditation trying to imagine himself as waves. He thought of many different things. Then gradually he turned more and more to the feeling of the waves. As the night advanced the waves became larger and larger. They swept away the flowers in their vases. Even the Buddha in the shrine was inundated. Before dawn the temple was nothing but the ebb and flow of an immense sea.

In the morning the teacher found O-nami meditating, a faint smile on his face. He patted the wrestler's shoulder. "Now nothing can disturb you," he said. "You are those waves. You will sweep everything before you."

The same day O-nami entered the wrestling contests and won. After that, no one in Japan was able to defeat him.

月 *9. The Moon Cannot Be Stolen*

RYOKAN, a Zen master, lived the simplest kind of life in a little hut at the foot of a mountain. One evening a thief visited the hut only to discover there was nothing in it to steal.

Ryokan returned and caught him. "You may have come a long way to visit me," he told the prowler, "and you should not return empty-handed. Please take my clothes as a gift."

The thief was bewildered. He took the clothes and slunk away.

Ryokan sat naked, watching the moon. "Poor fellow," he mused, "I wish I could give him this beautiful moon."

終 *10. The Last Poem of Hoshin*

THE ZEN MASTER Hoshin lived in China many years. Then he returned to the northeastern part of Japan, where he taught his disciples. When he was getting very old, he told them a story he had heard in China. This is the story:

One year on the twenty-fifth of December, Tokufu, who was very old, said to his disciples: "I am not going to be alive next year so you fellows should treat me well this year."

The pupils thought he was joking, but since he was a great-hearted teacher each of them in turn treated him to a feast on succeeding days of the departing year.

On the eve of the new year, Tokufu concluded: "You have been good to me. I shall leave you tomorrow afternoon when the snow has stopped."

The disciples laughed, thinking he was aging and talking nonsense since the night was clear and without snow. But at midnight snow began to fall, and the next day they did not find their teacher about. They went to the meditation hall. There he had passed on.

Hoshin, who related this story, told his disciples: "It is not necessary for a Zen master to predict his passing, but if he really wishes to do so, he can."

"Can you ?" someone asked.

"Yes," answered Hoshin. "I will show you what I can do seven days from now."

None of the disciples believed him, and most of them had even forgotten the conversation when Hoshin next called them together.

"Seven days ago," he remarked, "I said I was going to leave you. It is customary to write a farewell poem, but I am neither poet nor calligrapher. Let one of you inscribe my last words."

His followers thought he was joking, but one of them started to write.

"Are you ready?" Hoshin asked.

"Yes, sir," replied the writer.

Then Hoshin dictated:

> *I came from brilliancy*
> *And return to brilliancy.*
> *What is this?*

The poem was one line short of the customary four, so the disciple said: "Master, we are one line short."

Hoshin, with the roar of a conquering lion, shouted "Kaa!" and was gone.

# 忘 11. The Story of Shunkai

THE EXQUISITE Shunkai whose other name was Suzu was compelled to marry against her wishes when she was quite young. Later, after this marriage had ended, she attended the university, where she studied philosophy.

To see Shunkai was to fall in love with her. Moreover, wherever she went, she herself fell in love with others. Love was with her at the university, and afterwards, when philosophy did not satisfy her and she visited a temple to learn about Zen, the Zen students fell in love with her. Shunkai's whole life was saturated with love.

At last in Kyoto she became a real student of Zen. Her brothers in the sub-temple of Kennin praised her sincerity. One of them proved to be a congenial spirit and assisted her in the mastery of Zen.

The abbot of Kennin, Mokurai, Silent Thunder, was severe. He kept the precepts himself and expected his priests to do so. In modern Japan whatever zeal these priests have lost for Buddhism they seem to have gained for having wives. Mokurai used to take a broom and chase the women away when he found them in any of his temples, but the more wives he swept out, the more seemed to come back.

In this particular temple the wife of the head priest became jealous of Shunkai's earnestness and beauty. Hearing the students praise her serious Zen made this wife squirm and itch. Finally she spread a rumor about Shunkai and the young man who was her friend. As a consequence he was expelled and Shunkai was removed from the temple.

"I may have made the mistake of love," thought Shunkai, "but the priest's wife shall not remain in the temple either if my friend is to be treated so unjustly."

Shunkai the same night with a can of kerosene set fire to the five-hundred-year-old temple and burned it to the ground. In the morning she found herself in the hands of the police.

A young lawyer became interested in her and endeavored to make her sentence lighter. "Do not help me," she told him. "I might decide to do something else which would only imprison me again."

At last a sentence of seven years was completed, and Shunkai was released from the prison, where the sixty-year-old warden also had become enamored of her.

But now everyone looked upon her as a "jailbird." No one would associate with her. Even the Zen people, who are supposed to believe in enlightenment in this life and with this body, shunned her. Zen, Shunkai found, was one thing and the followers of Zen quite another. Her relatives would have nothing to do with her. She grew sick, poor, and weak.

She met a Shinshu priest who taught her the name of the Buddha of Love, and in this Shunkai found some solace and peace of mind. She passed away when she was still exquisitely beautiful and hardly thirty years old.

She wrote her own story in a futile endeavor to support herself and some of it she told to a woman writer. So it reached the Japanese people. Those who rejected Shunkai, those who slandered and hated her, now read of her life with tears of remorse.

# 福 12. Happy Chinaman

ANYONE WALKING about Chinatowns in America will observe statues of a stout fellow carrying a linen sack. Chinese merchants call him Happy Chinaman or Laughing Buddha.

This Hotei lived in the T'ang dynasty. He had no desire to call himself a Zen master or to gather many disciples about him. Instead he walked the streets with a big sack into which he would put gifts of candy, fruit, or doughnuts. These he would give to children who gathered around him in play. He established a kindergarten of the streets.

Whenever he met a Zen devotee he would extend his hand and say: "Give me one penny." And if anyone asked him to return to a temple to teach others, again he would reply: "Give me one penny."

Once as he was about his play-work another Zen master happened along and inquired: "What is the significance of Zen?"

Hotei immediately plopped his sack down on the ground in silent answer.

"Then," asked the other, "what is the actualization of Zen?"

At once the Happy Chinaman swung the sack over his shoulder and continued on his way.

# 佛 13. A Buddha

IN TOKYO in the Meiji era there lived two prominent teachers of opposite characteristics. One, Unsho, an instructor in Shingon, kept Buddha's precepts scrupulously. He never drank intoxicants, nor did he eat after eleven o'clock in the morning. The other teacher, Tanzan, a professor of philosophy at the Imperial University, never observed the precepts. When he felt like eating he ate, and when he felt like sleeping in the daytime he slept.

One day Unsho visited Tanzan, who was drinking wine at the time, not even a drop of which is supposed to touch the tongue of a Buddhist.

"Hello, brother," Tanzan greeted him. "Won't you have a drink?"

"I never drink!" exclaimed Unsho solemnly.

"One who does not drink is not even human," said Tanzan.

"Do you mean to call me inhuman just because I do not indulge in intoxicating liquids!" exclaimed Unsho in anger. "Then if I am not human, what am I?"

"A Buddha," answered Tanzan.

難 *14. Muddy Road*

TANZAN AND EKIDO were once traveling together down a muddy road. A heavy rain was still falling.

Coming around a bend, they met a lovely girl in a silk kimono and sash, unable to cross the intersection.

"Come on, girl," said Tanzan at once. Lifting her in his arms, he carried her over the mud.

Ekido did not speak again until that night when they reached a lodging temple. Then he no longer could restrain himself. "We monks don't go near females," he told Tanzan, "especially not young and lovely ones. It is dangerous. Why did you do that?"

"I left the girl there," said Tanzan. "Are you still carrying her?"


親 *15. Shoun & His Mother*

SHOUN BECAME a teacher of Soto Zen. When he was still a student his father passed away, leaving him to care for his old mother.

Whenever Shoun went to a meditation hall he always took his mother with him. Since she accompanied him, when he visited monasteries he could not live with the monks. So he would build a little house and care for her there. He would copy sutras, Buddhist verses, and in this manner receive a few coins for food.

When Shoun bought fish for his mother, the people would scoff at him, for a monk is not supposed to eat fish. But Shoun did not mind. His mother, however, was hurt to see others laugh at her son. Finally she told Shoun: "I think I will become a nun. I can be a vegetarian too." She did, and they studied together.

Shoun was fond of music and was a master of the harp, which his mother also played. On full moon nights they used to play together.

One night a young lady passed by their house and heard music. Deeply touched, she invited Shoun to visit her the next evening and play. He accepted the invitation. A few days later he met the young lady on the street and thanked her for her hospitality. Others laughed at him. He had visited the house of a woman of the streets.

One day Shoun left for a distant temple to deliver a lecture. A few months afterwards he returned home to find his mother dead. Friends had not known where to reach him, so the funeral was then in progress.

Shoun walked up and hit the coffin with his staff. "Mother, your son has returned," he said.

"I am glad to see you have returned, son," he answered for his mother.

"Yes, I'm glad too," Shoun responded. Then he announced to the people about him: "The funeral ceremony is over. You may bury the body."

When Shoun was old he knew his end was approaching. He asked his disciples to gather around him in the morning, telling them he was going to pass on at noon. Burning incense before the picture of his mother and his old teacher, he wrote a poem:

> *For fifty-six years I lived as best I could,*
> *Making my way in this world.*
> *Now the rain has ended, the clouds are clearing*
> *The blue sky has a full moon.*

His disciples gathered about him, reciting a sutra, and Shoun passed on during the invocation.

## 王 16. Not Far from Buddhahood

A UNIVERSITY STUDENT while visiting Gasan asked him: "Have you ever read the Christian Bible?"

"No, read it to me," said Gasan.

The student opened the Bible and read from St. Matthew: "And why take ye thought for raiment? Consider the lilies of the field, how they grow. They toil not, neither do they spin, and yet I say unto you that even Solomon in all his glory was not arrayed like one of these....Take therefore no thought for the morrow, for the morrow shall take thought for the things of itself."

Gasan said: "Whoever uttered those words I consider an enlightened man."

The student continued reading: "Ask and it shall be given you, seek and ye shall find, knock and it shall be opened unto you. For everyone that asketh receiveth, and he that seeketh findeth, and to him that knocketh, it shall be opened." Gasan remarked: "That is excellent. Whoever said that is not far from Buddhahood."

## 教 17. Stingy in Teaching

A YOUNG PHYSICIAN in Tokyo named Kusuda met a college friend who had been studying Zen. The young doctor asked him what Zen was.

"I cannot tell you what it is," the friend replied, "but one thing is certain. If you understand Zen, you will not be afraid to die."

"That's fine," said Kusuda. "I will try it. Where can I find a teacher?"

"Go to the master Nan-in," the friend told him.

So Kusuda went to call on Nan-in. He carried a dagger nine and a half inches long to determine whether or not the teacher himself was afraid to die.

When Nan-in saw Kusuda he exclaimed: "Hello, friend. How are you? We haven't seen each other for a long time!"

This perplexed Kusuda, who replied: "We have never met before."

"That's right," answered Nan-in. "I mistook you for another physician who is receiving instruction here."

With such a beginning, Kusuda lost his chance to test the master, so reluctantly he asked if he might receive Zen instruction.

Nan-in said: "Zen is not a difficult task. If you are a physician, treat your patients with kindness. That is Zen."

Kusuda visited Nan-in three times. Each time Nan-in told him the same thing. "A physician should not waste time around here. Go home and take care of your patients."

It was not yet clear to Kusuda how such teaching could remove the fear of death. So on his fourth visit he complained: "My friend told me that when one learns Zen one loses his fear of death. Each time I come here all you tell me is to take care of my patients. I know that much. If that is your so-called Zen, I am not going to visit you any more."

Nan-in smiled and patted the doctor. "I have been too strict with you. Let me give you a koan." He presented Kusuda with Joshu's Mu to work over, which is the first mind-enlightening problem in the book called *The Gateless Gate*.

Kusuda pondered this problem of Mu (No-Thing) for two years. At length he thought he had reached certainty of mind. But his teacher commented: "You are not in yet."

Kusuda continued in concentration for another year and a half. His mind became placid. Problems dissolved. No-Thing became the truth. He served his patients well and, without even knowing it, he was free from concern over life and death.

Then when he visited Nan-in, his old teacher just smiled.

# 絶 18. A Parable

BUDDHA TOLD a parable in a sutra:

A man traveling across a field encountered a tiger. He fled, the tiger after him. Coming to a precipice, he caught hold of the root of a wild vine and swung himself down over the edge. The tiger sniffed at him from above. Trembling, the man looked down to where, far below, another tiger was waiting to eat him. Only the vine sustained him.

Two mice, one white and one black, little by little started to gnaw away the vine. The man saw a luscious strawberry near him. Grasping the vine with one hand, he plucked the strawberry with the other. How sweet it tasted!

陣 *19. The First Principle*

WHEN ONE GOES to Obaku temple in Kyoto he sees carved over the gate the words "The First Principle." The letters are unusually large, and those who appreciate calligraphy always admire them as being a masterpiece. They were drawn by Kosen two hundred years ago.

When the master drew them he did so on paper, from which workmen made the larger carving in wood. As Kosen sketched the letters a bold pupil was with him who had made several gallons of ink for the calligraphy and who never failed to criticize his master's work.

"That is not good," he told Kosen after the first effort.

"How is that one?"

"Poor. Worse than before," pronounced the pupil.

Kosen patiently wrote one sheet after another until eighty-four First Principles had accumulated, still without the approval of the pupil.

Then, when the young man stepped outside for a few moments, Kosen thought: "Now is my chance to escape his keen eye," and he wrote hurriedly, with a mind free from distraction: "The First Principle."

"A masterpiece," pronounced the pupil.

## 㐱 20. A Mother's Advice

JIUN, A SHINGON MASTER, was a well-known Sanskrit scholar of the Tokugawa era. When he was young he used to deliver lectures to his brother students.

His mother heard about this and wrote him a letter:

"Son, I do not think you became a devotee of the Buddha because you desired to turn into a walking dictionary for others. There is no end to information and commentation, glory and honor. I wish you would stop this lecture business. Shut yourself up in a little temple in a remote part of the mountain. Devote your time to meditation and in this way attain true realization."


## 音 21. The Sound of One Hand

THE MASTER of Kennin temple was Mokurai, Silent Thunder. He had a little protege named Toyo who was only twelve years old. Toyo saw the older disciples visit the master's room each morning and evening to receive instruction in sanzen or personal guidance in which they were given koans to stop mind-wandering.

Toyo wished to do sanzen also.

"Wait a while," said Mokurai. "You are too young."

But the child insisted, so the teacher finally consented.

In the evening little Toyo went at the proper time to the threshold of Mokurai's sanzen room. He struck the gong to announce his presence, bowed respectfully three times outside the door, and went to sit before the master in respectful silence.

"You can hear the sound of two hands when they clap together," said Mokurai. "Now show me the sound of one hand."

Toyo bowed and went to his room to consider this problem. From his window he could hear the music of the geishas. "Ah, I have it!" he proclaimed.

The next evening, when his teacher asked him to illustrate the sound of one hand, Toyo began to play the music of the geishas.

"No, no," said Mokurai. "That will never do. That is not the sound of one hand. You've not got it at all."

Thinking that such music might interrupt, Toyo moved his abode to a quiet place. He meditated again. "What can the sound of one hand be?" He happened to hear some water dripping. "I have it," imagined Toyo.

When he next appeared before his teacher, Toyo imitated dripping water.

"What is that?" asked Mokurai. "That is the sound of dripping water, but not the sound of one hand. Try again."

In vain Toyo meditated to hear the sound of one hand. He heard the sighing of the wind. But the sound was rejected.

He heard the cry of an owl. This also was refused. The sound of one hand was not the locusts.

For more than ten times Toyo visited Mokurai with different sounds. All were wrong. For almost a year he pondered what the sound of one hand might be.

At last little Toyo entered true meditation and transcended all sounds. "I could collect no more," he explained later, "so I reached the soundless sound."

Toyo had realized the sound of one hand.

# 炎 22. My Heart Burns Like Fire

SOYEN SHAKU, the first Zen teacher to come to America, said: "My heart burns like fire but my eyes are as cold as dead ashes." He made the following rules which he practiced every day of his life.

In the morning before dressing, light incense and meditate.

Retire at a regular hour. Partake of food at regular intervals. Eat with moderation and never to the point of satisfaction.

Receive a guest with the same attitude you have when alone. When alone, maintain the same attitude you have in receiving guests.

Watch what you say, and whatever you say, practice it.

When an opportunity comes do not let it pass by, yet always think twice before acting.

Do not regret the past. Look to the future.

Have the fearless attitude of a hero and the loving heart of a child.

Upon retiring, sleep as if you had entered your last sleep. Upon awakening, leave your bed behind you instantly as if you had cast away a pair of old shoes.

## 煙 23. Eshun's Departure

WHEN ESHUN, the Zen nun, was past sixty and about to leave this world, she asked some monks to pile up wood in the yard.

Seating herself firmly in the center of the funeral pyre, she had it set fire around the edges.

"O nun!" shouted one monk, "is it hot in there?" "Such a matter would concern only a stupid person like yourself," answered Eshun. The flames arose, and she passed away.

# 經 24. Reciting Sutras

A FARMER requested a Tendai priest to recite sutras for his wife, who had died. After the recitation was over the farmer asked: "Do you think my wife will gain merit from this?"

"Not only your wife, but all sentient beings will benefit from the recitation of sutras," answered the priest.

"If you say all sentient beings will benefit," said the farmer, "my wife may be very weak and others will take advantage of her, getting the benefit she should have. So please recite sutras just for her."

The priest explained that it was the desire of a Buddhist to offer blessings and wish merit for every living being.

"That is a fine teaching," concluded the farmer, "but please make one exception. I have a neighbor who is rough and mean to me. Just exclude him from all those sentient beings."

余 *25. Three Days More*

SUIWO, THE DISCIPLE of Hakuin, was a good teacher. During one summer seclusion period, a pupil came to him from a southern island of Japan.

Suiwo gave him the problem: "Hear the sound of one hand."

The pupil remained three years but could not pass this test. One night he came in tears to Suiwo. "I must return south in shame and embarrassment," he said, "for I cannot solve my problem."

"Wait one week more and meditate constantly," advised Suiwo. Still no enlightenment came to the pupil. "Try for another week," said Suiwo. The pupil obeyed, but in vain.

"Still another week." Yet this was of no avail. In despair the student begged to be released, but Suiwo requested another meditation of five days. They were without result. Then he said: "Meditate for three days longer, then if you fail to attain enlightenment, you had better kill yourself."

On the second day the pupil was enlightened.

# 盲 26. Trading Dialogue for Lodging

PROVIDED HE MAKES and wins an argument about Buddhism with those who live there, any wandering monk can remain in a Zen temple. If he is defeated, he has to move on.

In a temple in the northern part of Japan two brother monks were dwelling together. The elder one was learned, but the younger one was stupid and had but one eye.

A wandering monk came and asked for lodging, properly challenging them to a debate about the sublime teaching. The elder brother, tired that day from much studying, told the younger one to take his place. "Go and request the dialogue in silence," he cautioned.

So the young monk and the stranger went to the shrine and sat down.

Shortly afterwards the traveler rose and went in to the elder brother and said: "Your young brother is a wonderful fellow. He defeated me."

"Relate the dialogue to me," said the elder one.

"Well," explained the traveler, "first I held up one finger, representing Buddha, the enlightened one. So he held up two fingers, signifying Buddha and his teaching. I held up three fingers, representing Buddha, his teaching, and his followers, living the harmonious life. Then he shook his clenched fist in my face, indicating that all three come from one realization. Thus he won and so I have no right to remain here." With this, the traveler left.

"Where is that fellow?" asked the younger one, running in to his elder brother.

"I understand you won the debate."

"Won nothing. I'm going to beat him up."

"Tell me the subject of the debate," asked the elder one.

"Why, the minute he saw me he held up one finger, insulting me by insinuating that I have only one eye. Since he was a stranger I thought I would be polite to him, so I held up two fingers, congratulating him that he has two eyes. Then the impolite wretch held up three fingers, suggesting that between us we only have three eyes. So I got mad and started to punch him, but he ran out and that ended it!"

誠 27. The Voice of Happiness

AFTER BANKEI had passed away, a blind man who lived near the master's temple told a friend: "Since I am blind, I cannot watch a person's face, so I must judge his character by the sound of his voice. Ordinarily when I hear someone congratulate another upon his happiness or success, I also hear a secret tone of envy. When condolence is expressed for the misfortune of another, I hear pleasure and satisfaction, as if the one condoling was really glad there was something left to gain in his own world.

"In all my experience, however, Bankei's voice was always sincere. Whenever he expressed happiness, I heard nothing but happiness, and whenever he expressed sorrow, sorrow was all I heard."

# 藏 28. Open Your Own Treasure House

DAIJU VISITED the master Baso in China. Baso asked: "What do you seek?"

"Enlightenment," replied Daiju.

"You have your own treasure house. Why do you search outside?" Baso asked.

Daiju inquired: "Where is my treasure house?"

Baso answered: "What you are asking is your treasure house."

Daiju was enlightened! Ever after he urged his friends: "Open your own treasure house and use those treasures."

# 影 29. No Water, No Moon

WHEN THE NUN Chiyono studied Zen under Bukko of Engaku she was unable to attain the fruits of meditation for a long time.

At last one moonlit night she was carrying water in an old pail bound with bamboo. The bamboo broke and the bottom fell out of the pail, and at that moment Chiyono was set free!

In commemoration, she wrote a poem:

> *In this way and that I tried to save the old pail*
> *Since the bamboo strip was weakening and about to*
>     *break*
> *Until at last the bottom fell out.*
> *No more water in the pail!*
> *No more moon in the water!*

# 位 30. Calling Card

KEICHU, THE GREAT Zen teacher of the Meiji era, was the head of Tofuku, a cathedral in Kyoto. One day the governor of Kyoto called upon him for the first time.

His attendant presented the card of the governor, which read: Kitagaki, Governor of Kyoto.

"I have no business with such a fellow," said Keichu to his attendant. "Tell him to get out of here."

The attendant carried the card back with apologies. "That was my error," said the governor, and with a pencil he scratched out the words Governor of Kyoto. "Ask your teacher again."

"Oh, is that Kitagaki?" exclaimed the teacher when he saw the card. "I want to see that fellow."

# 優 31. Everything Is Best

WHEN BANZAN was walking through a market he overheard a conversation between a butcher and his customer.

"Give me the best piece of meat you have," said the customer.

"Everything in my shop is the best," replied the butcher. "You cannot find here any piece of meat that is not the best."

At these words Banzan became enlightened.

時 *32. Inch Time Foot Gem*

A LORD ASKED Takuan, a Zen teacher, to suggest how he might pass the time. He felt his days very long attending his office and sitting stiffly to receive the homage of others.

Takuan wrote eight Chinese characters and gave them to the man:

> *Not twice this day*
> *Inch time foot gem.*
> *This day will not come again.*
> *Each minute is worth a priceless gem.*

握 *33. Mokusen's Hand*

MOKUSEN HIKI was living in a temple in the province of Tamba. One of his adherents complained of the stinginess of his wife.

Mokusen visited the adherent's wife and showed her his clenched fist before her face.

"What do you mean by that?" asked the surprised woman.

"Suppose my fist were always like that. What would you call it?" he asked.

"Deformed," replied the woman.

Then he opened his hand flat in her face and asked: "Suppose it were always like that. What then?"

"Another kind of deformity," said the wife.

"If you understand that much," finished Mokusen, "you are a good wife." Then he left.

After his visit, this wife helped her husband to distribute as well as to save.


# 笑 34. A Smile in His Lifetime

MOKUGEN WAS never known to smile until his last day on earth. When his time came to pass away he said to his faithful ones: "You have studied under me for more than ten years. Show me your real interpretation of Zen. Whoever expresses this most clearly shall be my successor and receive my robe and bowl."

Everyone watched Mokugen's severe face, but no one answered.

Encho, a disciple who had been with his teacher for a long time, moved near the bedside. He pushed forward the medicine cup a few inches. This was his answer to the command.

The teacher's face became even more severe. "Is that all you understand?" he asked.

Encho reached out and moved the cup back again.

A beautiful smile broke over the features of Moku-gen. "You rascal," he told Encho. "You worked with me ten years and have not yet seen my whole body. Take the robe and bowl. They belong to you."

## 維 35. Every-Minute Zen

ZEN STUDENTS are with their masters at least ten years before they presume to teach others. Nan-in was visited by Tenno, who, having passed his apprentice-ship, had become a teacher. The day happened to be rainy, so Tenno wore wooden clogs and carried an umbrella. After greeting him Nan-in remarked: "I suppose you left your wooden clogs in the vestibule. I want to know if your umbrella is on the right or left side of the clogs."

Tenno, confused, had no instant answer. He realized that he was unable to carry his Zen every minute. He became Nan-in's pupil, and he studied six more years to accomplish his every-minute Zen.

# 花 36. Flower Shower

SUBHUTI WAS Buddha's disciple. He was able to understand the potency of emptiness, the viewpoint that nothing exists except in its relationship of subjectivity and objectivity.

One day Subhuti, in a mood of sublime emptiness, was sitting under a tree. Flowers began to fall about him.

"We are praising you for your discourse on emptiness," the gods whispered to him.

"But I have not spoken of emptiness," said Subhuti.

"You have not spoken of emptiness, we have not heard emptiness," responded the gods. "This is the true emptiness." And blossoms showered upon Subhuti as rain.

# 救 37. Publishing the Sutras

TETSUGEN, A DEVOTEE of Zen in Japan, decided to publish the sutras, which at that time were available only in Chinese. The books were to be printed with wood blocks in an edition of seven thousand copies, a tremendous undertaking.

Tetsugen began by traveling and collecting donations for this purpose. A few sympathizers would give him a hundred pieces of gold, but most of the time he received only small coins. He thanked each donor with equal gratitude. After ten years Tetsugen had enough money to begin his task.

It happened that at that time the Uji River overflowed. Famine followed. Tetsugen took the funds he had collected for the books and spent them to save others from starvation. Then he began again his work of collecting.

Several years afterwards an epidemic spread over the country. Tetsugen again gave away what he had collected, to help his people.

For a third time he started his work, and after twenty years his wish was fulfilled. The printing blocks that produced the first edition of sutras can be seen today in the Obaku monastery in Kyoto.

The Japanese tell their children that Tetsugen made three sets of sutras, and that the first two invisible sets surpass even the last.

# 㠭 38. Gisho's Work

GISHO WAS ordained as a nun when she was ten years old. She received training just as the little boys did. When she reached the age of the sixteen she traveled from one Zen master to another, studying with them all.

She remained three years with Unzan, six years with Gukei, but was unable to obtain a clear vision. At last she went to the master Inzan.

Inzan showed her no distinction at all on account of her sex. He scolded her like a thunderstorm. He cuffed her to awaken her inner nature.

Gisho remained with Inzan thirteen years, and then she found that which she was seeking!

In her honor, Inzan wrote a poem:

> This nun studied thirteen years under my
>     guidance.
> In the evening she considered the deepest koans,
> In the morning she was wrapped in other koans.
> The Chinese nun Tetsuma surpassed all before her,
> And since Mujaku none has been so genuine as
>     this Gisho!
> Yet there are many more gates for her to
>     pass through.
> She should receive still more blows from my
>     iron fist.

After Gisho was enlightened she went to the province of Banshu, started her own Zen temple, and taught two hundred other nuns until she passed away one year in the month of August.

## 怠 39. Sleeping in the Daytime

THE MASTER Soyen Shaku passed from this world when he was sixty-one years of age. Fulfilling his life's work, he left a great teaching, far richer than that of most Zen masters. His pupils used to sleep in the daytime during midsummer, and while he overlooked this he himself never wasted a minute.

When he was but twelve years old he was already studying Tendai philosophical speculation. One summer day the air had been so sultry that little Soyen stretched his legs and went to sleep while his teacher was away.

Three hours passed when, suddenly waking, he heard his master enter, but it was too late. There he lay, sprawled across the doorway.

"I beg your pardon, I beg your pardon," his teacher whispered, stepping carefully over Soyen's body as if it were that of some distinguished guest. After this, Soyen never slept again in the afternoon.

夢 *40. In Dreamland*

"OUR SCHOOLMASTER used to take a nap every afternoon," related a disciple of Soyen Shaku. "We children asked him why he did it and he told us: 'I go to dreamland to meet the old sages just as Confucius did.' When Confucius slept, he would dream of ancient sages and later tell his followers about them.

"It was extremely hot one day so some of us took a nap. Our schoolmaster scolded us. 'We went to dreamland to meet the ancient sages the same as Confucius did,' we explained. 'What was the message from those sages?' our schoolmaster demanded. One of us replied: 'We went to dreamland and met the sages and asked them if our schoolmaster came there every afternoon, but they said they had never seen any such fellow.'"

捨 *41. Joshu's Zen*

JOSHU BEGAN the study of Zen when he was sixty years old and continued until he was eighty, when he realized Zen.

He taught from the age of eighty until he was one hundred and twenty.

A student once asked him: "If I haven't anything in my mind, what shall I do?"

Joshu replied: "Throw it out."

"But if I haven't anything, how can I throw it out?" continued the questioner.

"Well," said Joshu, "then carry it out."

# 擬 42. The Dead Man's Answer

WHEN MAMIYA, who later became a well-known preacher, went to a teacher for personal guidance, he was asked to explain the sound of one hand.

Mamiya concentrated upon what the sound of one hand might be. "You are not working hard enough," his teacher told him. "You are too attached to food, wealth, things, and that sound. It would be better if you died. That would solve the problem."

The next time Mamiya appeared before his teacher he was again asked what he had to show regarding the sound of one hand. Mamiya at once fell over as if he were dead.

"You are dead all right," observed the teacher. "But how about that sound?"

"I haven't solved that yet," replied Mamiya, looking up.

"Dead men do not speak," said the teacher. "Get out!"

# 賤 43. Zen in a Beggar's Life

TOSUI WAS a well-known Zen teacher of his time. He had lived in several temples and taught in various provinces.

The last temple he visited accumulated so many adherents that Tosui told them he was going to quit the lecture business entirely. He advised them to disperse and to go wherever they desired. After that no one could find any trace of him.

Three years later one of his disciples discovered him living with some beggars under a bridge in Kyoto. He at once implored Tosui to teach him.

"If you can do as I do for even a couple of days, I might," Tosui replied.

So the former disciple dressed as a beggar and spent a day with Tosui. The following day one of the beggars died. Tosui and his pupil carried the body off at midnight and buried it on a mountainside. After that they returned to their shelter under the bridge.

Tosui slept soundly the remainder of the night, but the disciple could not sleep. When morning came Tosui said: "We do not have to beg food today. Our dead friend has left some over there." But the disciple was unable to eat a single bite of it.

"I have said you could not do as I," concluded Tosui. "Get out of here and do not bother me again."

悟
賊 *44. The Thief Who
Became a Disciple*

ONE EVENING as Shichiri Kojun was reciting sutras a thief with a sharp sword entered, demanding either his money or his life.

Shichiri told him: "Do not disturb me. You can find the money in that drawer." Then he resumed his recitation.

A little while afterwards he stopped and called:

"Don't take it all. I need some to pay taxes with tomorrow."

The intruder gathered up most of the money and started to leave. "Thank a person when you receive a gift," Shichiri added. The man thanked him and made off.

A few days afterwards the fellow was caught and confessed, among others, the offence against Shichiri. When Shichiri was called as a witness he said: "This man is no thief, at least as far as I am concerned. I gave him the money and he thanked me for it."

After he had finished his prison term, the man went to Shichiri and became his disciple.

盗 *45. Right & Wrong*

WHEN BANKEI held his seclusion-weeks of meditation, pupils from many parts of Japan came to attend. During one of these gatherings a pupil was caught stealing. The matter was reported to Bankei with the request that the culprit be expelled. Bankei ignored the case.

Later the pupil was caught in a similar act, and again Bankei disregarded the matter. This angered the other pupils, who drew up a petition asking for the dismissal of the thief, stating that otherwise they would leave in a body.

When Bankei had read the petition he called everyone before him. "You are wise brothers," he told them. "You know what is right and what is not right. You may go somewhere else to study if you wish, but this poor brother does not even know right from wrong. Who will teach him if I do not? I am going to keep him here even if all the rest of you leave."

A torrent of tears cleansed the face of the brother who had stolen. All desire to steal had vanished.

草
木
## 46. How Grass & Trees Become Enlightened

DURING THE Kamakura period, Shinkan studied Tendai six years and then studied Zen seven years; then he went to China and contemplated Zen for thirteen years more.

When he returned to Japan many desired to interview him and asked obscure questions. But when Shinkan received visitors, which was infrequently, he seldom answered their questions.

One day a fifty-year-old student of enlightenment said to Shinkan: "I have studied the Tendai school of thought since I was a little boy, but one thing in it I cannot understand. Tendai claims that even the grass and trees will become enlightened. To me this seems very strange."

"Of what use is it to discuss how grass and trees become enlightened?" asked Shinkan. "The question is how you yourself can become so. Did you ever consider that?"

"I never thought of it in that way," marveled the old man.

"Then go home and think it over," finished Shinkan.

# 畫 47. The Stingy Artist

GESSEN WAS an artist monk. Before he would start a drawing or painting he always insisted upon being paid in advance, and his fees were high. He was known as the "Stingy Artist."

A geisha once gave him a commission for a painting. "How much can you pay?" inquired Gessen.

"Whatever you charge," replied the girl, "but I want you to do the work in front of me."

So on a certain day Gessen was called by the geisha. She was holding a feast for her patron.

Gessen with fine brushwork did the painting. When it was completed he asked the highest sum of his time.

He received his pay. Then the geisha turned to her patron, saying: "All this artist wants is money. His paintings are fine but his mind is dirty; money has caused it to become muddy. Drawn by such a filthy mind, his work is not fit to exhibit. It is just about good enough for one of my petticoats."

Removing her skirt, she then asked Gessen to do another picture on the back of her petticoat.

"How much will you pay?" asked Gessen.

"Oh, any amount," answered the girl.

Gessen named a fancy price, painted the picture in the manner requested, and went away.

It was learned later that Gessen had these reasons for desiring money:

A ravaging famine often visited his province. The rich would not help the poor, so Gessen had a secret warehouse, unknown to anyone, which he kept filled with grain, prepared for these emergencies.

From his village to the National Shrine the road was in very poor condition and many travelers suffered while traversing it. He desired to build a better road.

His teacher had passed away without realizing his wish to build a temple, and Gessen wished to complete this temple for him.

After Gessen had accomplished his three wishes he threw away his brushes and artist's materials and, retiring to the mountains, never painted again.

# 衡 48. Accurate Proportion

SEN NO RIKYU, a tea-master, wished to hang a flower basket on a column. He asked a carpenter to help him, directing the man to place it a little higher or lower, to the right or left, until he had found exactly the right spot. "That's the place," said Sen no Rikyu finally.

The carpenter, to test the master, marked the spot and then pretended he had forgotten. "Was this the place? Was this the place, perhaps?" the carpenter kept asking, pointing to various places on the column.

But so accurate was the tea-master's sense of proportion that it was not until the carpenter reached the identical spot again that its location was approved.

## 惡 49. Black-Nosed Buddha

A NUN WHO was searching for enlightenment made a statue of Buddha and covered it with gold leaf. Wherever she went she carried this golden Buddha with her.

Years passed and, still carrying her Buddha, the nun came to live in a small temple in a country where there were many Buddhas, each one with its own particular shrine.

The nun wished to burn incense before her golden Buddha. Not liking the idea of the perfume straying to the others, she devised a funnel through which the smoke would ascend only to her statue. This blackened the nose of the golden Buddha, making it especially ugly.

# 忘 50. *Ryonen's Clear Realization*

THE BUDDHIST NUN known as Ryonen was born in 1797. She was a granddaughter of the famous Japanese warrior Shingen. Her poetical genius and alluring beauty were such that at seventeen she was serving the empress as one of the ladies of the court. Even at such a youthful age fame awaited her.

The beloved empress died suddenly and Ryonen's hopeful dreams vanished. She became acutely aware of the impermanency of life in this world. It was then that she desired to study Zen.

Her relatives disagreed, however, and practically forced her into marriage. With a promise that she might become a nun after she had borne three children, Ryonen assented. Before she was twenty-five she had accomplished this condition. Then her husband and relatives could no longer dissuade her from her desire. She shaved her head, took the name of Ryonen, which means to realize clearly, and started on her pilgrimage.

She came to the city of Edo and asked Tetsugyu to accept her as a disciple. At one glance the master rejected her because she was too beautiful.

Ryonen then went to another master, Hakuo. Hakuo refused her for the same reason, saying that her beauty would only make trouble.

Ryonen obtained a hot iron and placed it against her face. In a few moments her beauty had vanished forever.

Hakuo then accepted her as a disciple. Commemorating this occasion, Ryonen wrote a poem on the back of a little mirror:

> *In the service of my Empress I burned incense*
> *to perfume my exquisite clothes,*
> *Now as a homeless mendicant I burn my face*
> *to enter a Zen temple.*

When Ryonen was about to pass from this world, she wrote another poem:

> *Sixty-six times have these eyes beheld the changing*
> *scene of autumn.*
> *I have said enough about moonlight,*
> *Ask no more.*
> *Only listen to the voice of pines and cedars when*
> *no wind stirs.*

**膳** *51. Sour Miso*

The cook monk Dairyo, at Bankei's monastery, decided that he would take good care of his old teacher's health and give him only fresh miso, a paste of soy beans mixed with wheat and yeast that often ferments. Bankei, noticing that he was being served better miso than his pupils, asked: "Who is the cook today?"

Dairyo was sent before him. Bankei learned that according to his age and position he should eat only fresh miso. So he said to the cook: "Then you think I shouldn't eat at all." With this he entered his room and locked the door.

Dairyo, sitting outside the door, asked his teacher's pardon. Bankei would not answer. For seven days Dairyo sat outside and Bankei within.

Finally in desperation an adherent called loudly to Bankei: "You may be all right, old teacher, but this young disciple here has to eat. He cannot go without food forever!"

At that Bankei opened the door. He was smiling. He told Dairyo: "I insist on eating the same food as the least of my followers. When you become the teacher I do not want you to forget this."

**滅** *52. Your Light May Go Out*

A STUDENT of Tendai, a philosophical school of Buddhism, came to the Zen abode of Gasan as a pupil. When he was departing a few years later, Gasan warned him: "Studying the truth speculatively is useful as a way of collecting preaching material. But remember that unless you meditate constantly your light of truth may go out."

**諜** *53. The Giver Should Be Thankful*

WHILE SEISETSU was the master of Engaku in Kamakura he required larger quarters, since those in which he was teaching were overcrowded. Umezu Seibei a merchant of Edo, decided to donate five hundred pieces of gold called ryo toward the construction of a more commodious school. This money he brought to the teacher.

Seisetsu said: "All right. I will take it."

Umezu gave Seisetsu the sack of gold, but he was dissatisfied with the attitude of the teacher. One might live a whole year on three ryo, and the merchant had not even been thanked for five hundred.

"In that sack are five hundred ryo," hinted Umezu.

"You told me that before," replied Seisetsu.

"Even if I am a wealthy merchant, five hundred ryo is a lot of money," said Umezu.

"Do you want me to thank you for it?" asked Seisetsu.

"You ought to," replied Umezu.

"Why should I?" inquired Seisetsu. "The giver should be thankful."

遺 54. *The Last Will & Testament*

IKKYU, A FAMOUS Zen teacher of the Ashikaga era, was the son of the emperor. When he was very young, his mother left the palace and went to study Zen in a temple. In this way Prince Ikkyu also became a student. When his mother passed on, she left with him a letter. It read:

*To Ikkyu:*

*I have finished my work in this life and am now returning into Eternity. I wish you to become a good student and to realize your Buddha-nature. You will know if I am in hell and whether I am always with you or not.*

*If you become a man who realizes that the Buddha and his follower Bodhidharma are your own servants, you may leave off studying and work for humanity. The Buddha preached for forty-nine years and in all that time found it*

*not necessary to speak one word. You ought to know why.*
*But if you don't and yet wish to, avoid thinking fruitlessly.*

> *Your Mother,*
> *Not born, not dead.*
> *September first.*

*P.S. The teaching of Buddha was mainly for the purpose*
*of enlightening others. If you are dependent on any of its*
*methods, you are naught but an ignorant insect. There are*
*80,000 books on Buddhism and if you should read all of*
*them and still not see your own nature, you will not under-*
*stand even this letter. This is my will and testament.*

殺
意
## 55. The Tea-Master & the Assassin

TAIKO, A WARRIOR who lived in Japan before the Tokugawa era, studied Cha-no-yu, tea etiquette, with Sen no Rikyu, a teacher of that aesthetical expression of calmness and contentment.

Taiko's attendant warrior Kato interpreted his superior's enthusiasm for tea etiquette as negligence of state affairs, so he decided to kill Sen no Rikyu. He pretended to make a social call upon the teamaster and was invited to drink tea.

The master, who was well skilled in his art, saw at a glance the warrior's intention, so he invited Kato to leave his sword outside before entering the room for the ceremony, explaining that Cha-no-yu represents peacefulness itself.

Kato would not listen to this. "I am a warrior," he said. "I always have my sword with me. Cha-no-yu or no Cha-no-yu, I have my sword."

"Very well. Bring your sword in and have some tea," consented Sen no Rikyu.

The kettle was boiling on the charcoal fire. Suddenly Sen no Rikyu tipped it over. Hissing steam arose, filling the room with smoke and ashes. The startled warrior ran outside.

The tea-master apologized. "It was my mistake. Come back in and have some tea. I have your sword here covered with ashes and will clean it and give it to you."

In this predicament the warrior realized he could not very well kill the tea-master, so he gave up the idea.


## 道 56. The True Path

JUST BEFORE Ninakawa passed away the Zen master Ikkyu visited him. "Shall I lead you on?" Ikkyu asked.

Ninakawa replied: "I came here alone and I go alone. What help could you be to me?"

Ikkyu answered: "If you think you really come and go, that is your delusion. Let me show you the path on which there is no coming and no going."

With his words, Ikkyu had revealed the path so clearly that Ninakawa smiled and passed away.

# 門 57. The Gates of Paradise

A SOLDIER NAMED Nobushige came to Hakuin, and asked: "Is there really a paradise and a hell?"

"Who are you?" inquired Hakuin.

"I am a samurai," the warrior replied.

"You, a soldier!" exclaimed Hakuin. "What kind of ruler would have you as his guard? Your face looks like that of a beggar."

Nobushige became so angry that he began to draw his sword, but Hakuin continued: "So you have a sword! Your weapon is probably much too dull to cut off my head."

As Nobushige drew his sword Hakuin remarked: "Here open the gates of hell!"

At these words the samurai, perceiving the master's discipline, sheathed his sword and bowed.

"Here open the gates of paradise," said Hakuin.

# 裁 58. Arresting the Stone Buddha

A MERCHANT bearing fifty rolls of cotton goods on his shoulders stopped to rest from the heat of the day beneath a shelter where a large stone Buddha was standing. There he fell asleep, and when he awoke his goods had disappeared. He immediately reported the matter to the police.

A judge named O-oka opened court to investigate. "That stone Buddha must have stolen the goods," concluded the judge. "He is supposed to care for the welfare of the people, but he has failed to perform his holy duty. Arrest him."

The police arrested the stone Buddha and carried it into the court. A noisy crowd followed the statue, curious to learn what kind of a sentence the judge was about to impose.

When O-oka appeared on the bench he rebuked the boisterous audience. "What right have you people to appear before the court laughing and joking in this manner? You are in contempt of court and subject to a fine and imprisonment."

The people hastened to apologize. "I shall have to impose a fine on you," said the judge, "but I will remit it provided each one of you brings one roll of cotton goods to the court within three days. Anyone failing to do this will be arrested."

One of the rolls of cloth that the people brought was quickly recognized by the merchant as his own, and thus the thief was easily discovered. The merchant recovered his goods, and the cotton rolls were returned to the people.

## 將 59. Soldiers of Humanity

ONCE A DIVISION of the Japanese army was engaged in a sham battle, and some of the officers found it necessary to make their headquarters in Gasan's temple.

Gasan told his cook: "Let the officers have only the same simple fare we eat."

This made the army men angry, as they were used to very deferential treatment. One came to Gasan and said: "Who do you think we are? We are soldiers, sacrificing our lives for our country. Why don't you treat us accordingly?"

Gasan answered sternly: "Who do you think we are? We are soldiers of humanity, aiming to save all sentient beings."

# 路 60. The Tunnel

ZENKAI, THE SON of a samurai, journeyed to Edo and there became the retainer of a high official. He fell in love with the official's wife and was discovered. In self-defence, he slew the official. Then he ran away with the wife.

Both of them later became thieves. But the woman was so greedy that Zenkai grew disgusted. Finally, leaving her, he journeyed far away to the province of Buzen, where he became a wandering mendicant.

To atone for his past, Zenkai resolved to accomplish some good deed in his lifetime. Knowing of a dangerous road over a cliff that had caused the death and injury of many persons, he resolved to cut a tunnel through the mountain there.

Begging food in the daytime, Zenkai worked at night digging his tunnel. When thirty years had gone by, the tunnel was 2,280 feet long, 20 feet high, and 30 feet wide.

Two years before the work was completed, the son of the official he had slain, who was a skillful swordsman, found Zenkai out and came to kill him in revenge.

"I will give you my life willingly," said Zenkai. "Only let me finish this work. On the day it is completed, then you may kill me."

So the son awaited the day. Several months passed and Zenkai kept on digging. The son grew tired of doing nothing and began to help with the digging. After he had helped for more than a year, he came to admire Zenkai's strong will and character.

At last the tunnel was completed and the people could use it and travel in safety.

"Now cut off my head," said Zenkai. "My work is done."

"How can I cut off my own teacher's head?" asked the younger man with tears in his eyes.

# 師 61. Gudo and the Emperor

THE EMPEROR Goyozei was studying Zen under Gudo. He inquired: "In Zen this very mind is Buddha. Is this correct?"

Gudo answered: "If I say yes, you will think that you understand without understanding. If I say no, I would be contradicting a fact which many understand quite well."

On another day the emperor asked Gudo: "Where does the enlightened man go when he dies?"

Gudo answered: "I know not."

"Why don't you know?" asked the emperor.

"Because I have not died yet," replied Gudo.

The emperor hesitated to inquire further about these things his mind could not grasp. So Gudo beat the floor with his hand as if to awaken him, and the emperor was enlightened!

The emperor respected Zen and old Gudo more than ever after his enlightenment, and he even permitted Gudo to wear his hat in the palace in winter. When Gudo was over eighty he used to fall asleep in the midst of his lecture, and the emperor would quietly retire to another room so his beloved teacher might enjoy the rest his aging body required.

運 ## 62. In the Hands of Destiny

A GREAT JAPANESE warrior named Nobunaga decided to attack the enemy although he had only one-tenth the number of men the opposition commanded. He knew that he would win, but his soldiers were in doubt.

On the way he stopped at a Shinto shrine and told his men: "After I visit the shrine I will toss a coin. If heads comes, we will win; if tails, we will lose. Destiny holds us in her hand."

Nobunaga entered the shrine and offered a silent prayer. He came forth and tossed a coin. Heads appeared. His soldiers were so eager to fight that they won their battle easily.

"No one can change the hand of destiny," his attendant told him after the battle.

"Indeed not," said Nobunaga, showing a coin that had been doubled, with heads facing either way.

亡 63. Killing

Gasan instructed his adherents one day: "Those who speak against killing and who desire to spare the lives of all conscious beings are right. It is good to protect even animals and insects. But what about those persons who kill time, what about those who are destroying wealth, and those who destroy political economy? We should not overlook them. Furthermore, what of the one who preaches without enlightenment? He is killing Buddhism."

几 64. Kasan Sweat

KASAN WAS asked to officiate at the funeral of a provincial lord.

He had never met lords and nobles before so he was nervous. When the ceremony started, Kasan sweat.

Afterwards, when he had returned, he gathered his pupils together. Kasan confessed that he was not yet qualified to be a teacher for he lacked the sameness of bearing in the world of fame that he possessed in the secluded temple. Then Kasan resigned and became the pupil of another master. Eight years later he returned to his former pupils, enlightened.

## 恰 65. The Subjugation of a Ghost

A YOUNG WIFE fell sick and was about to die. "I love you so much," she told her husband, "I do not want to leave you. Do not go from me to any other woman. If you do, I will return as a ghost and cause you endless trouble."

Soon the wife passed away. The husband respected her last wish for the first three months, but then he met another woman and fell in love with her. They became engaged to be married.

Immediately after the engagement a ghost appeared every night to the man, blaming him for not keeping his promise. The ghost was clever too. She told him exactly what had transpired between himself and his new sweetheart. Whenever he gave his fiancée a present, the ghost would describe it in detail. She would even repeat conversations, and it so annoyed the man that he could not sleep. Someone advised him to take his problem to a Zen master who lived close to the village. At length, in despair, the poor man went to him for help.

"Your former wife became a ghost and knows everything you do," commented the master. "Whatever you do or say, whatever you give your beloved, she knows. She must be a very wise ghost. Really you should admire such a ghost. The next time she appears, bargain with her. Tell her that she knows so much you can hide nothing from her, and that if she will answer you one question, you promise to break your engagement and remain single."

"What is the question I must ask her?" inquired the man.

The master replied: "Take a large handful of soy beans and ask her exactly how many beans you hold in your hand. If she cannot tell you, you will know she is only a figment of your imagination and will trouble you no longer."

The next night, when the ghost appeared the man flattered her and told her that she knew everything.

"Indeed," replied the ghost, "and I know you went to see that Zen master today."

"And since you know so much," demanded the man, "tell me how many beans I hold in this hand!"

There was no longer any ghost to answer the question.

**耶** *66. Children of His Majesty*

YAMAOKA TESSHU was a tutor of the emperor. He was also a master of fencing and a profound student of Zen.

His home was the abode of vagabonds. He had but one suit of clothes, for they kept him always poor.

The emperor, observing how worn his garments were, gave Yamaoka some money to buy new ones. The next time Yamaoka appeared he wore the same old outfit.

"What became of the new clothes, Yamaoka?" asked the emperor.

"I provided clothes for the children of Your Majesty," explained Yamaoka.


**何** *67. What Are You Doing!*
**語** *What Are You Saying!*

IN MODERN TIMES a great deal of nonsense is talked about masters and disciples, and about the inheritance of a master's teaching by favorite pupils, entitling them to pass the truth on to their adherents. Of course Zen should be imparted in this way, from heart to heart, and in the past it was really accomplished. Silence and humility reigned rather than profession and assertion. The one who received such a teaching kept the matter hidden even after twenty years. Not until another discovered through his own need that a real master was at hand was it learned that the teaching had been imparted, and even then the occasion arose quite naturally and the teaching made its way in its own right. Under no circumstance did the teacher even claim "I am the successor of So-and-so." Such a claim would prove quite the contrary. The Zen master Mu-nan had only one successor. His name was Shoju. After Shoju had completed his study of Zen, Mu-nan called him into his room. "I am getting old," he said, "and as far as I know, Shoju, you are the only one who will carry on this teaching. Here is a book. It has been passed down from master to master for seven generations. I also have added many points according to my understanding. The book is very valuable, and I am giving it to you to represent your successorship."

"If the book is such an important thing, you had better keep it," Shoju replied. "I received your Zen without writing and am satisfied with it as it is."

"I know that," said Mu-nan. "Even so, this work has been carried from master to master for seven generations, so you may keep it as a symbol of having received the teaching. Here."

The two happened to be talking before a brazier. The instant Shoju felt the book in his hands he thrust it into the flaming coals. He had no lust for possessions.

Mu-nan, who never had been angry before, yelled: "What are you doing!"

Shoju shouted back: "What are you saying!"

## 笛 68. One Note of Zen

AFTER KAKUA visited the emperor he disappeared and no one knew what became of him. He was the first Japanese to study Zen in China, but since he showed nothing of it, save one note, he is not remembered for having brought Zen into his country.

Kakua visited China and accepted the true teaching. He did not travel while he was there. Meditating constantly, he lived on a remote part of a mountain. Whenever people found him and asked him to preach he would say a few words and then move to another part of the mountain where he could be found less easily.

The emperor heard about Kakua when he returned to Japan and asked him to preach Zen for his edification and that of his subjects.

Kakua stood before the emperor in silence. He then produced a flute from the folds of his robe, and blew one short note. Bowing politely, he disappeared.

**罪** *69. Eating the Blame*

CIRCUMSTANCES AROSE one day which delayed preparation of the dinner of a Soto Zen master, Fugai, and his followers. In haste the cook went to the garden with his curved knife and cut off the tops of green vegetables, chopped them together, and made soup, unaware that in his haste he had included a part of a snake in the vegetables. The followers of Fugai thought they never had tasted such good soup. But when the master himself found the snake's head in his bowl, he summoned the cook. "What is this?" he demanded, holding up the head of the snake.

"Oh, thank you, master," replied the cook, taking the morsel and eating it quickly.

**猫**
**頭** *70. The Most Valuable Thing in the World*

SOZAN, A CHINESE Zen master, was asked by a student: "What is the most valuable thing in the world?"

The master replied: "The head of a dead cat." "Why is the head of a dead cat the most valuable thing in the world?" inquired the student.

Sozan replied: "Because no one can name its price."

## 默 71. Learning To Be Silent

THE PUPILS of the Tendai school used to study meditation before Zen entered Japan. Four of them who were intimate friends promised one another to observe seven days of silence.

On the first day all were silent. Their meditation had begun auspiciously, but when night came and the oil lamps were growing dim one of the pupils could not help exclaiming to a servant: "Fix those lamps."

The second pupil was surprised to hear the first one talk. "We are not supposed to say a word," he remarked.

"You two are stupid. Why did you talk?" asked the third.

"I am the only one who has not talked," concluded the fourth pupil.

## 愚 72. The Blockhead Lord

TWO ZEN TEACHERS, Daigu and Gudo, were invited to visit a lord. Upon arriving, Gudo said to the lord: "You are wise by nature and have an inborn ability to learn Zen."

"Nonsense," said Daigu. "Why do you flatter this blockhead? He may be a lord, but he doesn't know anything of Zen."

So, instead of building a temple for Gudo, the lord built it for Daigu and studied Zen with him.

## 従 73. Ten Successors

ZEN PUPILS take a vow that even if they are killed by their teacher, they intend to learn Zen. Usually they cut a finger and seal their resolution with blood. In time the vow has become a mere formality, and for this reason the pupil who died by the hand of Ekido was made to appear a martyr.

Ekido had become a severe teacher. His pupils feared him. One of them on duty, striking the gong to tell the time of day, missed his beats when his eye was attracted by a beautiful girl passing the temple gate.

At that moment Ekido, who was directly behind him, hit him with a stick and the shock happened to kill him.

The pupil's guardian, hearing of the accident, went directly to Ekido. Knowing that he was not to blame, he praised the master for his severe teaching. Ekido's attitude was just the same as if the pupil were still alive.

After this took place, he was able to produce under his guidance more than ten enlightened successors, a very unusual number.

## 戒 74. True Reformation

RYOKAN DEVOTED his life to the study of Zen. One day he heard that his nephew, despite the admonitions of relatives, was spending his money on a courtesan. Inasmuch as the nephew had taken Ryokan's place in managing the family estate and the property was in danger of being dissipated, the relatives asked Ryokan to do something about it.

Ryokan had to travel a long way to visit his nephew, whom he had not seen for many years. The nephew seemed pleased to meet his uncle again and invited him to remain overnight.

All night Ryokan sat in meditation. As he was departing in the morning he said to the young man: "I must be getting old, my hand shakes so. Will you help me tie the string of my straw sandal?"

The nephew helped him willingly. "Thank you," finished Ryokan, "you see, a man becomes older and feebler day by day. Take good care of yourself." Then Ryokan left, never mentioning a word about the courtesan or the complaints of the relatives. But, from that morning on, the dissipations of the nephew ended.

氣 75. *Temper*

A ZEN STUDENT came to Bankei and complained: "Master, I have an ungovernable temper. How can I cure it?"

"You have something very strange," replied Bankei. "Let me see what you have."

"Just now I cannot show it to you," replied the other.

"When can you show it to me?" asked Bankei.

"It arises unexpectedly," replied the student.

"Then," concluded Bankei, "it must not be your own true nature. If it were, you could show it to me at any time. When you were born you did not have it, and your parents did not give it to you. Think that over."

**岩** *76. The Stone Mind*

HOGEN, A CHINESE Zen teacher, lived alone in a small temple in the country. One day four traveling monks appeared and asked if they might make a fire in his yard to warm themselves.

While they were building the fire, Hogen heard them arguing about subjectivity and objectivity. He joined them and said: "There is a big stone. Do you consider it to be inside or outside your mind?"

One of the monks replied: "From the Buddhist viewpoint everything is an objectification of mind, so I would say that the stone is inside my mind."

"Your head must feel very heavy," observed Hogen, "if you are carrying around a stone like that in your mind."

**煩** *77. No Attachment to Dust*

ZENGETSU, A CHINESE master of the T'ang dynasty, wrote the following advice for his pupils: Living in the world yet not forming attachments to the dust of the world is the way of a true Zen student.

When witnessing the good action of another encourage yourself to follow his example. Hearing of the mistaken action of another, advise yourself not to emulate it.

Even though alone in a dark room, be as if you were facing a noble guest. Express your feelings, but become no more expressive than your true nature.

Poverty is your treasure. Never exchange it for an easy life.

A person may appear a fool and yet not be one. He may only be guarding his wisdom carefully.

Virtues are the fruit of self-discipline and do not drop from heaven of themselves as does rain or snow.

Modesty is the foundation of all virtues. Let your neighbors discover you before you make yourself known to them.

A noble heart never forces itself forward. Its words are as rare gems, seldom displayed and of great value.

To a sincere student, every day is a fortunate day. Time passes but he never lags behind. Neither glory nor shame can move him.

Censure yourself, never another. Do not discuss right and wrong.

Some things, though right, were considered wrong for generations. Since the value of righteousness may be recognized after centuries, there is no need to crave an immediate appreciation.

Live with cause and leave results to the great law of the universe. Pass each day in peaceful contemplation.

# 榮 78. Real Prosperity

A RICH MAN asked Sengai to write something for the continued prosperity of his family so that it might be treasured from generation to generation.

Sengai obtained a large sheet of paper and wrote: "Father dies, son dies, grandson dies."

The rich man became angry. "I asked you to write something for the happiness of my family! Why do you make such a joke as this?"

"No joke is intended," explained Sengai. "If before you yourself die your son should die, this would grieve you greatly. If your grandson should pass away before your son, both of you would be broken-hearted. If your family, generation after generation, passes away in the order I have named, it will be the natural course of life. I call this real prosperity."

# 造 79 Incense Burner

A WOMAN OF NAGASAKI named Kame was one of the few makers of incense burners in Japan. Such a burner is a work of art to be used only in a tearoom or before a family shrine.

Kame, whose father before her had been such an artist, was fond of drinking. She also smoked and associated with men most of the time. Whenever she made a little money she gave a feast inviting artists, poets, carpenters, workers, men of many vocations and avocations. In their association she evolved her designs.

Kame was exceedingly slow in creating, but when her work was finished it was always a masterpiece. Her burners were treasured in homes whose womenfolk never drank, smoked, or associated freely with men.

The mayor of Nagasaki once requested Kame to design an incense burner for him. She delayed doing so until almost half a year had passed. At that time the mayor, who had been promoted to office in a distant city, visited her. He urged Kame to begin work on his burner.

At last receiving the inspiration, Kame made the incense burner. After it was completed she placed it upon a table. She looked at it long and carefully. She smoked and drank before it as if it were her own company. All day she observed it.

At last, picking up a hammer, Kame smashed it to bits. She saw it was not the perfect creation her mind demanded.

# 律 80. The Real Miracle

WHEN BANKEI was preaching at Ryumon temple, a Shinshu priest, who believed in salvation through the repetition of the name of the Buddha of Love, was jealous of his large audience and wanted to debate with him.

Bankei was in the midst of a talk when the priest appeared, but the fellow made such a disturbance that Bankei stopped his discourse and asked about the noise.

"The founder of our sect," boasted the priest, "had such miraculous powers that he held a brush in his hand on one bank of the river, his attendant held up a paper on the other bank, and the teacher wrote the holy name of Amida through the air. Can you do such a wonderful thing?"

Bankei replied lightly: "Perhaps your fox can perform that trick, but that is not the manner of Zen. My miracle is that when I feel hungry I eat, and when I feel thirsty I drink."

# 靜 81. Just Go To Sleep

GASAN WAS sitting at the bedside of Tekisui three days before his teacher's passing. Tekisui had already chosen him as his successor.

A temple recently had burned and Gasan was busy rebuilding the structure. Tekisui asked him: "What are you going to do when you get the temple rebuilt?"

"When your sickness is over we want you to speak there," said Gasan.

"Suppose I do not live until then?"

"Then we will get someone else," replied Gasan.

"Suppose you cannot find anyone?" continued Tekisui.

Gasan answered loudly: "Don't ask such foolish questions. Just go to sleep."

# 無 82. Nothing Exists

YAMAOKA TESSHU, AS a young student of Zen, visited one master after another. He called upon Dokuon of Shokoku.

Desiring to show his attainment, he said: "The mind, Buddha, and sentient beings, after all, do not exist. The true nature of phenomena is emptiness.

There is no realization, no delusion, no sage, no mediocrity. There is no giving and nothing to be received."

Dokuon, who was smoking quietly, said nothing. Suddenly he whacked Yamaoka with his bamboo pipe. This made the youth quite angry.

"If nothing exists," inquired Dokuon, "where did this anger come from?"

## 饡 83. No Work, No Food

HYAKUJO, THE CHINESE Zen master, used to labor with his pupils even at the age of eighty, trimming the gardens, cleaning the grounds, and pruning the trees.

The pupils felt sorry to see the old teacher working so hard, but they knew he would not listen to their advice to stop, so they hid away his tools.

That day the master did not eat. The next day he did not eat, nor the next. "He may be angry because we have hidden his tools," the pupils surmised. "We had better put them back."

The day they did, the teacher worked and ate the same as before. In the evening he instructed them: "No work, no food."

# 絃 84. True Friends

A LONG TIME AGO in China there were two friends, one who played the harp skillfully and one who listened skillfully.

When the one played or sang about a mountain, the other would say: "I can see the mountain before us."

When the one played about water, the listener would exclaim: "Here is the running stream!"

But the listener fell sick and died. The first friend cut the strings of his harp and never played again. Since that time the cutting of harp strings has always been a sign of intimate friendship.

# 期 85. Time To Die

IKKYU, THE Zen master, was very clever even as a boy. His teacher had a precious teacup, a rare antique. Ikkyu happened to break this cup and was greatly perplexed. Hearing the footsteps of his teacher, he held the pieces of the cup behind him. When the master appeared, Ikkyu asked: "Why do people have to die?"

"This is natural," explained the older man. "Everything has to die and has just so long to live."

Ikkyu, producing the shattered cup, added: "It was time for your cup to die."

樽
屋 *86. The Living Buddha*
*& the Tubmaker*

ZEN MASTERS GIVE personal guidance in a secluded room. No one enters while teacher and pupil are together.

Mokurai, the Zen master of Kennin temple in Kyoto, used to enjoy talking with merchants and newspapermen as well as with his pupils. A certain tubmaker was almost illiterate. He would ask foolish questions of Mokurai, have tea, and then go away.

One day while the tubmaker was there Mokurai wished to give personal guidance to a disciple, so he asked the tubmaker to wait in another room.

"I understand you are a living Buddha," the man protested. "Even the stone Buddhas in the temple never refuse the numerous persons who come together before them. Why then should I be excluded?"

Mokurai had to go outside to see his disciple.

# 學 87. Three Kinds of Disciples

A ZEN MASTER named Gettan lived in the latter part of the Tokugawa era. He used to say: "There are three kinds of disciples: those who impart Zen to others, those who maintain the temples and shrines, and then there are the rice bags and the clothes-hangers."

Gasan expressed the same idea. When he was studying under Tekisui, his teacher was very severe. Sometimes he even beat him. Other pupils would not stand this kind of teaching and quit. Gasan remained, saying: "A poor disciple utilizes a teacher's influence. A fair disciple admires a teacher's kindness. A good disciple grows strong under a teacher's discipline."

# 詩 88. How To Write a Chinese Poem

A WELL-KNOWN Japanese poet was asked how to compose a Chinese poem.

"The usual Chinese poem is four lines," he explained. "The first line contains the initial phase; the second line, the continuation of that phase; the third line turns from this subject and begins a new one; and the fourth line brings the first three lines together. A popular Japanese song illustrates this:

*Two daughters of a silk merchant live in Kyoto.*
*The elder is twenty, the younger, eighteen.*
*A soldier may kill with his sword,*
*But these girls slay men with their eyes."*

# 問 89. Zen Dialogue

ZEN TEACHERS train their young pupils to express themselves. Two Zen temples each had a child protégé. One child, going to obtain vegetables each morning, would meet the other on the way.

"Where are you going?" asked the one.

"I am going wherever my feet go," the other responded.

This reply puzzled the first child who went to his teacher for help. "Tomorrow morning," the teacher told him, "when you meet that little fellow, ask him the same question. He will give you the same answer, and then you ask him: 'Suppose you have no feet, then where are you going?' That will fix him."

The children met again the following morning.

"Where are you going?" asked the first child.

"I am going wherever the wind blows," answered the other.

This again nonplussed the youngster, who took his defeat to his teacher.

"Ask him where he is going if there is no wind," suggested the teacher.

The next day the children met a third time.

"Where are you going?" asked the first child.

"I am going to market to buy vegetables," the other replied.

## 許 90. The Last Rap

TANGEN HAD STUDIED with Sengai since childhood. When he was twenty he wanted to leave his teacher and visit others for comparative study, but Sengai would not permit this. Every time Tangen suggested it, Sengai would give him a rap on the head.

Finally Tangen asked an elder brother to coax permission from Sengai. This the brother did and then reported to Tangen: "It is arranged. I have fixed it for you to start on your pilgrimage at once."

Tangen went to Sengai to thank him for his permission. The master answered by giving him another rap.

When Tangen related this to his elder brother the other said: "What is the matter? Sengai has no business giving permission and then changing his mind. I will tell him so." And off he went to see the teacher.

"I did not cancel my permission," said Sengai. "I just wished to give him one last smack over the head, for when he returns he will be enlightened and I will not be able to reprimand him again."

## 毅 91. *The Taste of Banzo's Sword*

MATAJURO YAGYU was the son of a famous swordsman. His father, believing that his son's work was too mediocre to anticipate mastership, disowned him.

So Matajuro went to Mount Futara and there found the famous swordsman Banzo. But Banzo confirmed the father's judgment. "You wish to learn swordsmanship under my guidance?" asked Banzo. "You cannot fulfill the requirements."

"But if I work hard, how many years will it take me to become a master?" persisted the youth.

"The rest of your life," replied Banzo.

"I cannot wait that long," explained Matajuro. "I am willing to pass through any hardship if only you will teach me. If I become your devoted servant, how long might it be?"

"Oh, maybe ten years," Banzo relented.

"My father is getting old, and soon I must take care of him," continued Matajuro. "If I work far more intensively, how long would it take me?"

"Oh, maybe thirty years," said Banzo.

"Why is that?" asked Matajuro. "First you say ten and now thirty years. I will undergo any hardship to master this art in the shortest time!"

"Well," said Banzo, "in that case you will have to remain with me for seventy years. A man in such a hurry as you are to get results seldom learns quickly."

"Very well," declared the youth, understanding at last that he was being rebuked for impatience, "I agree."

Matajuro was told never to speak of fencing and never to touch a sword. He cooked for his master, washed the dishes, made his bed, cleaned the yard, cared for the garden, all without a word of swordsmanship.

Three years passed. Still Matajuro labored on. Thinking of his future, he was sad. He had not even begun to learn the art to which he had devoted his life.

But one day Banzo crept up behind him and gave him a terrific blow with a wooden sword.

The following day, when Matajuro was cooking rice, Banzo again sprang upon him unexpectedly.

After that, day and night, Matajuro had to defend himself from unexpected thrusts. Not a moment passed in any day that he did not have to think of the taste of Banzo's sword.

He learned so rapidly he brought smiles to the face of his master. Matajuro became the greatest swordsman in the land.

**突** *92. Fire-Poker Zen*

HAKUIN USED to tell his pupils about an old woman who had a teashop, praising her understanding of Zen. The pupils refused to believe what he told them and would go to the teashop to find out for themselves.

Whenever the woman saw them coming she could tell at once whether they had come for tea or to look into her grasp of Zen. In the former case, she would serve them graciously. In the latter, she would beckon to the pupils to come behind her screen. The instant they obeyed, she would strike them with a fire-poker.

Nine out of ten of them could not escape her beating.

**語** *93. Storyteller's Zen*

ENCHO WAS a famous storyteller. His tales of love stirred the hearts of his listeners. When he narrated a story of war, it was as if the listeners themselves were on the field of battle.

One day Encho met Yamaoka Tesshu, a layman who had almost embraced masterhood in Zen. "I understand," said Yamaoka, "you are the best storyteller in our land and that you make people cry or laugh at will. Tell me my favorite story of the Peach Boy. When I was a little tot I used to sleep beside my mother, and she often related this legend. In the middle of the story I would fall asleep. Tell it to me just as my mother did."

Encho dared not attempt to do this. He requested time to study. Several months later he went to Yamaoka and said: "Please give me the opportunity to tell you the story."

"Some other day," answered Yamaoka.

Encho was keenly disappointed. He studied further and tried again. Yamaoka rejected him many times. When Encho would start to talk Yamaoka would stop him, saying: "You are not yet like my mother."

It took Encho five years to be able to tell Yamaoka the legend as his mother had told it to him.

In this way, Yamaoka imparted Zen to Encho.

忍 *94. Midnight Excursion*

MANY PUPILS were studying meditation under the Zen master Sengai. One of them used to arise at night, climb over the temple wall, and go to town on a pleasure jaunt.

Sengai, inspecting the dormitory quarters, found this pupil missing one night and also discovered the high stool he had used to scale the wall. Sengai removed the stool and stood there in its place.

When the wanderer returned, not knowing that Sengai was the stool, he put his feet on the master's head and jumped down into the grounds. Discovering what he had done, he was aghast.

Sengai said: "It is very chilly in the early morning. Do be careful not to catch cold yourself."

The pupil never went out at night again.

## 雪 95. A Letter to a Dying Man

BASSUI WROTE the following letter to one of his disciples who was about to die:

"The essence of your mind is not born, so it will never die. It is not an existence, which is perishable. It is not an emptiness, which is a mere void. It has neither color nor form. It enjoys no pleasures and suffers no pains.

"I know you are very ill. Like a good Zen student, you are facing that sickness squarely. You may not know exactly who is suffering, but question yourself: What is the essence of this mind? Think only of this. You will need no more. Covet nothing. Your end which is endless is as a snowflake dissolving in the pure air."

# 水 96. A Drop of Water

A ZEN MASTER named Gisan asked a young student to bring him a pail of water to cool his bath.

The student brought the water and, after cooling the bath, threw on to the ground the little that was left over.

"You dunce!" the master scolded him. "Why didn't you give the rest of the water to the plants? What right have you to waste even a drop of water in this temple?"

The young student attained Zen in that instant. He changed his name to Tekisui, which means a drop of water.

# 究 97. Teaching the Ultimate

IN EARLY TIMES in Japan, bamboo-and-paper lanterns were used with candles inside. A blind man, visiting a friend one night, was offered a lantern to carry home with him.

"I do not need a lantern," he said. "Darkness or light is all the same to me."

"I know you do not need a lantern to find your way," his friend replied," but if you don't have one, someone else may run into you. So you must take it."

The blind man started off with the lantern and before he had walked very far someone ran squarely into him. "Look out where you are going!" he exclaimed to the stranger. "Can't you see this lantern?"

"Your candle has burned out, brother," replied the stranger.

書 *98. Non-Attachment*

KITANO GEMPO, abbot of Eihei temple, was ninety-two years old when he passed away in the year 1933. He endeavored his whole life not to be attached to anything. As a wandering mendicant when he was twenty he happened to meet a traveler who smoked tobacco. As they walked together down a mountain road, they stopped under a tree to rest. The traveler offered Kitano a smoke, which he accepted, as he was very hungry at the time.

"How pleasant this smoking is," he commented. The other gave him an extra pipe and tobacco and they parted.

Kitano felt: "Such pleasant things may disturb meditation. Before this goes too far, I will stop now." So he threw the smoking outfit away.

When he was twenty-three years old he studied *I'King*, the profoundest doctrine of the universe. It was winter at the time and he needed some heavy clothes. He wrote his teacher, who lived a hundred miles away, telling him of his need, and gave the letter to a traveler to deliver. Almost the whole winter passed and neither answer nor clothes arrived. So Kitano resorted to the prescience of *I-King*, which also teaches the art of divination, to determine whether or not his letter had miscarried. He found that this had been the case. A letter afterwards from his teacher made no mention of clothes.

"If I perform such accurate determinative work with *I-King*, I may neglect my meditation," felt Kitano. So he gave up this marvelous teaching and never resorted to its powers again.

When he was twenty-eight he studied Chinese calligraphy and poetry. He grew so skillful in these arts that his teacher praised him. Kitano mused: "If I don't stop now, I'll be a poet, not a Zen teacher." So he never wrote another poem.

# 獨 99. Tosui's Vinegar

TOSUI WAS the Zen master who left the formalism of temples to live under a bridge with beggars.

When he was getting very old, a friend helped him to earn his living without begging. He showed Tosui how to collect rice and manufacture vinegar from it, and Tosui did this until he passed away.

While Tosui was making vinegar, one of the beggars gave him a picture of the Buddha. Tosui hung it on the wall of his hut and put a sign beside it. The sign read:

"Mr. Amida Buddha: This little room is quite narrow. I can let you remain as a transient. But don't think I am asking you to help me to be reborn in your paradise."

## 默 *100. The Silent Temple*

SHOICHI WAS a one-eyed teacher of Zen, sparkling with enlightenment. He taught his disciples in Tofuku temple.

Day and night the whole temple stood in silence. There was no sound at all.

Even the reciting of sutras was abolished by the teacher. His pupils had nothing to do but meditate.

When the master passed away, an old neighbor heard the ringing of bells and the recitation of sutras. Then she knew Shoichi had gone.

禪 *101. Buddha's Zen*

BUDDHA SAID: "I consider the positions of kings and rulers as that of dust motes. I observe treasures of gold and gems as so many bricks and pebbles. I look upon the finest silken robes as tattered rags. I see myriad worlds of the universe as small seeds of fruit, and the greatest lake in India as a drop of oil on my foot. I perceive the teachings of the world to be the illusion of magicians. I discern the highest conception of emancipation as a golden brocade in a dream, and view the holy path of the illuminated ones as flowers appearing in one's eyes. I see meditation as a pillar of a mountain, Nirvana as a nightmare of daytime. I look upon the judgment of right and wrong as the serpentine dance of a dragon, and the rise and fall of beliefs as but traces left by the four seasons."

# THE GATELESS GATE

**by Ekai, called Mu-mon**

*Transcribed by Nyogen Senzaki and Paul Reps*

IF YOU like sweets and easy living, skip this book. It is about men tremendously intent on being reborn, on satori, enlightenment.

It can happen to you. In a flashing moment something opens. You are new all through. You see the same unsame world with fresh eyes.

This universe-renewing power comes by grace, not logic. Whatever you do or wherever you are seems to make little difference. It doesn't make sense. It makes you.

These old Chinese devised problems, called koan, to stop their students' word-drunkenness and mind-wandering. When they had the student meditate on a koan, this was another way of saying: Don't waste your life merely sensing; channel thought and feeling to one purpose—and then let it happen.

Has this art of turning on one's light been lost? It needn't be if you put your mind—and all else you have—to it. If the leaders of mankind were more aware, when by chance they come into minor powers they might exploit others less.

*These old teachers complimented their students by criticism, blows even. When they praised, it usually meant belittling. This was the custom. They had a deep concern for their pupils but showed it in presence, not words.*

*They were strong fellows, shockers. They gave questions for which the only answer was one's whole being.*

*What is the right answer to a koan? There are many right answers and there are also none. There is even a book in Japan, hard to come by, which gives proper answers to each of these mind-openers. What a joke!*

*For the koan itself is the answer, and by the time there is a right answer to it Zen is dead.*

*The following is adapted from the preface to the first English-language edition of this book.*

*The teaching of the Buddha was spread in India five hundred years prior to the time of Jesus and a thousand years before Mohammed. Buddhism joined the current of great faiths of the world long before Christianity and Islam.*

*Buddhist scriptures were translated into Chinese by both Indian and Chinese translators, dynasty after dynasty, from the first century of the Christian era. The essence of Buddhism, however, was carried from India to China in A.D. 520 by Bodhidharma, known as the first Zen patriarch. The wisdom of enlightenment generated from the Buddha by the silent-sitting Bodhidharma was inherited by his successor, and similarly handed down through many generations. It was thus that Zen entered, was nurtured in, and spread through China and eventually Japan.*

*The Japanese word* Zen—Ch'an *in Chinese,* Dhyana *in Sanskrit—means meditation. Zen aims, through meditation, to realize what Buddha himself realized, the emancipation of one's mind. It offers a method of selfsearching, usually under the personal guidance of a master.*

*Zen has many classic texts, of which this work is one.* Mu-mon-kan—*literally, "no gate barrier"—was recorded by the Chinese master Ekai, also called Mu-mon, who lived from 1183 to 1260. The work consists of narrated relationships between ancient Chinese teachers and their pupils, illustrating means employed to sublimate the dualistic, outgoing, generalizing, intellectualizing tendencies of students in order that they might realize their true nature. The problems or inner challenges with which the masters confronted their pupils came to be called koans, and each of the following stories is a koan in itself.*

*The stories use slang freely to actualize the highest teaching, the seeing into one's being. Occasional instances of apparent violence might be better interpreted as vigor and earnestness. None of the stories make any pretense at logic. They are dealing with states of mind rather than words. Unless this is understood, the point of the classic will be missed. The whole intent was to help the pupil break the shell of his limited mind and attain a second eternal birth,* satori, *enlightenment.*

*Each problem is a barrier. Those who have the spirit of Zen pass through it. Those who live in Zen understand one koan after another, each in his own way, as if they were seeing the unseen and living in the illimitable.*

Mu-mon wrote the following words in his introduction to the work.

"Zen has no gates. The purpose of Buddha's words is to enlighten others. Therefore Zen should be gateless.

"Now, how does one pass through this gateless gate? Some say that whatever enters through a gate is not family treasure, that whatever is produced by the help of another is likely to dissolve and perish.

"Even such words are like raising waves in a windless sea or performing an operation upon a healthy body. If one clings to what others have said and tries to understand Zen by explanation, he is like a dunce who thinks he can beat the moon with a pole or scratch an itching foot from the outside of a shoe. It will be impossible after all.

"In the year 1228 I was lecturing monks in the Ryusho temple in eastern China, and at their request I retold old koans, endeavoring to inspire their Zen spirit. I meant to use the koans as a man who picks up a piece of brick to knock at a gate, and after the gate is opened the brick is useless and is thrown away. My notes, however, were collected unexpectedly, and there were forty-eight koans, together with my comment in prose and verse concerning each, although their arrangement was not in the order of the telling. I have called the book The Gateless Gate, wishing students to read it as a guide.

"If a reader is brave enough and goes straight forward in his meditation, no delusions can disturb him. He will become enlightened just as did the patriarchs in India and in China, probably even better. But if he hesitates one moment,

*he is as a person watching from a small window for a horse-*
*man to pass by, and in a wink he has missed seeing.*

> *"The great path has no gates,*
> *Thousands of roads enter it.*
> *When one passes through this gateless gate*
> *He walks freely between heaven and earth."*

# 狗 *1. Joshu's Dog*

A MONK ASKED Joshu, a Chinese Zen master: "Has a dog Buddha-nature or not?"

Joshu answered: "Mu." (Mu is the negative symbol in Chinese, meaning "No thing" or "Nay.")

*Mumon's comment:* To realize Zen one has to pass through the barrier of the patriarchs. Enlightenment always comes after the road of thinking is blocked. If you do not pass the barrier of the patriarchs or if your thinking road is not blocked, whatever you think, whatever you do, is like a tangling ghost. You may ask: What is a barrier of a patriarch? This one word, Mu, is it.

This is the barrier of Zen. If you pass through it you will see Joshu face to face. Then you can work hand in hand with the whole line of patriarchs. Is this not a pleasant thing to do?

If you want to pass this barrier, you must work through every bone in your body, through every pore of your skin, filled with this question: What is Mu? and carry it day and night. Do not believe it is the common negative symbol meaning nothing. It is not nothingness, the opposite of existence. If you really want to pass this barrier, you should feel like drinking a hot iron ball that you can neither swallow nor spit out.

Then your previous lesser knowledge disappears. As a fruit ripening in season, your subjectivity and objectivity naturally become one. It is like a dumb man who has had a dream. He knows about it but he cannot tell it.

When he enters this condition his ego-shell is crushed and he can shake the heaven and move the earth. He is like a great warrior with a sharp sword. If a Buddha stands in his way, he will cut him down; if a patriarch offers him any obstacle, he will kill him; and he will be free in his way of birth and death. He can enter any world as if it were his own playground. I will tell you how to do this with this koan:

Just concentrate your whole energy into this Mu, and do not allow any discontinuation. When you enter this Mu and there is no discontinuation, your attainment will be as a candle burning and illuminating the whole universe.

> Has a dog Buddha-nature?
> This is the most serious question of all.
> If you say yes or no,
> You lose your own Buddha-nature.

# 狐 2. Hyakujo's Fox

ONCE WHEN HYAKUJO delivered some Zen lectures an old man attended them, unseen by the monks. At the end of each talk when the monks left so did he. But one day he remained after they had gone, and Hyakujo asked him: "Who are you?"

The old man replied: "I am not a human being, but I was a human being when the Kashapa Buddha preached in this world. I was a Zen master and lived on this mountain. At that time one of my students asked me whether or not the enlightened man is subject to the law of causation. I answered him: 'The enlightened man is not subject to the law of causation.' For this answer evidencing a clinging to absoluteness I became a fox for five hundred rebirths, and I am still a fox. Will you save me from this condition with your Zen words and let me get out of a fox's body? Now may I ask you: Is the enlightened man subject to the law of causation?"

Hyakujo said: "The enlightened man is one with the law of causation."

At the words of Hyakujo the old man was enlightened. "I am emancipated," he said, paying homage with a deep bow. "I am no more a fox, but I have to leave my body in my dwelling place behind this mountain. Please perform my funeral as a monk." Then he disappeared.

The next day Hyakujo gave an order through the chief monk to prepare to attend the funeral of a monk. "No one was sick in the infirmary," wondered the monks. "What does our teacher mean?"

After dinner Hyakujo led the monks out and a-round the mountain. In a cave, with his staff he poked out the corpse of an old fox and then performed the ceremony of cremation.

That evening Hyakujo gave a talk to the monks and told them this story about the law of causation.

Obaku, upon hearing the story, asked Hyakujo: "I understand that a long time ago because a certain person gave a wrong Zen answer he became a fox for five hundred rebirths. Now I want to ask: If some modern master is asked many questions and he always gives the right answer, what will become of him?"

Hyakujo said: "You come here near me and I will tell you."

Obaku went near Hyakujo and slapped the teacher's face with his hand, for he knew this was the answer his teacher intended to give him.

Hyakujo clapped his hands and laughed at this discernment. "I thought a Persian had a red beard," he said, "and now I know a Persian who has a red beard."

*Mumon's comment:* "The enlightened man is not subject." How can this answer make the monk a fox?

"The enlightened man is one with the law of causation." How can this answer make the fox emancipated? To understand this clearly one has to have just one eye.

> *Controlled or not controlled?*
> *The same dice shows two faces.*
> *Not controlled or controlled,*
> *Both are a grievous error.*

# 指 *3. Gutei's Finger*

GUTEI RAISED his finger whenever he was asked a question about Zen. A boy attendant began to imitate him in this way. When anyone asked the boy what his master had preached about, the boy would raise his finger.

Gutei heard about the boy's mischief. He seized him and cut off his finger. The boy cried and ran away. Gutei called and stopped him. When the boy turned his head to Gutei, Gutei raised up his own finger. In that instant the boy was enlightened.

When Gutei was about to pass from this world he gathered his monks around him. "I attained my finger-Zen," he said, "from my teacher Tenryu, and in my whole life I could not exhaust it." Then he passed away.

*Mumon's comment:* Enlightenment, which Gutei and the boy attained, has nothing to do with a finger. If anyone clings to a finger, Tenryu will be so disappointed that he will annihilate Gutei, the boy, and the finger all together.

> *Gutei cheapens the teaching of Tenryu,*
> *Emancipating the boy with a knife.*
> *Compared to the Chinese god who pushed*
>     *aside a mountain with one hand*
> *Old Gutei is a poor imitator.*

## 異 4. A Beardless Foreigner

WAKUAN COMPLAINED when he saw a picture of bearded Bodhidharma: "Why hasn't that fellow a beard?"

*Mumon's comment:* If you want to study Zen, you must study it with your heart. When you attain realization, it must be true realization. You yourself must have the face of the great Bodhidharma to see him. Just one such glimpse will be enough. But if you say you met him, you never saw him at all.

*One should not discuss a dream*
*In front of a simpleton.*
*Why has Bodhidharma no beard?*
*What an absurd question!*

## 落 5. Kyogen Mounts the Tree

KYOGEN SAID: "Zen is like a man hanging in a tree by his teeth over a precipice. His hands grasp no branch, his feet rest on no limb, and under the tree another person asks him: 'Why did Bodhidharma come to China from India?'

"If the man in the tree does not answer, he fails; and if he does answer, he falls and loses his life. Now what shall he do?"

*Mumon's comment:* In such a predicament the most talented eloquence is of no use. If you have memorized all the sutras, you cannot use them. When you can give the right answer, even though your past road was one of death, you open up a new road of life. But if you cannot answer, you should live ages hence and ask the future Buddha, Maitreya.

> *Kyogen is truly a fool*
> *Spreading that ego-killing poison*

*That closes his pupils' mouths*
*And lets their tears stream from their dead eyes.*

# 形 6. Buddha Twirls a Flower

WHEN BUDDHA was in Grdhrakuta Mountain he turned a flower in his fingers and held it before his listeners. Every one was silent. Only Maha-Kashapa smiled at this revelation, although he tried to control the lines of his face.

Buddha said: "I have the eye of the true teaching, the heart of Nirvana, the true aspect of non-form, and the ineffable stride of Dharma. It is not expressed by words, but especially transmitted beyond teaching. This teaching I have given to Maha-Kashapa."

*Mumon's comment:* Golden-faced Gautama thought he could cheat anyone. He made the good listeners as bad, and sold dog meat under the sign of mutton. And he himself thought it was wonderful. What if all the audience had laughed together? How could he have transmitted the teaching? And again, if Maha-Kashapa had not smiled, how could he have transmitted the teaching? If he says that realization can be transmitted, he is like the city slicker that cheats the country dub, and if he says it cannot be transmitted, why does he approve of Maha-Kashapa?

*At the turning of a flower*
*His disguise was exposed.*
*No one in heaven or earth can surpass*
*Maha-Kashapa's wrinkled face.*

## 洗 7. Joshu Washes the Bowl

A MONK TOLD JOSHU: "I have just entered the monastery. Please teach me."

Joshu asked: "Have you eaten your rice porridge?"

The monk replied: "I have eaten."

Joshu said: "Then you had better wash your bowl."

At that moment the monk was enlightened.

*Mumon's comment:* Joshu is the man who opens his mouth and shows his heart. I doubt if this monk really saw Joshu's heart. I hope he did not mistake the bell for a pitcher.

> *It is too clear and so it is hard to see.*
> *A dunce once searched for a fire with a*
> *    lighted lantern.*
> *Had he known what fire was,*
> *He could have cooked his rice much sooner.*

輪 *8. Keichu's Wheel*

GETSUAN SAID to his students: "Keichu, the first wheel-maker of China, made two wheels of fifty spokes each. Now, suppose you removed the nave uniting the spokes. What would become of the wheel? And had Keichu done this, could he be called the master wheel-maker?"

*Mumon's comment:* If anyone can answer this question instantly, his eyes will be like a comet and his mind like a flash of lightning.

> *When the hubless wheel turns,*
> *Master or no master can stop it.*
> *It turns above heaven and below earth,*
> *South, north, east, and west.*

聖 *9. A Buddha before History*

A MONK ASKED Seijo: "I understand that a Buddha who lived before recorded history sat in meditation for ten cycles of existence and could not realize the highest truth, and so could not become fully emancipated. Why was this so?" Seijo replied: "Your question is self-explanatory." The monk asked: "Since the Buddha was meditating, why could he not fulfill Buddhahood?" Seijo said: "He was not a Buddha."

*Mumon's comment:* I will allow his realization, but I will not admit his understanding. When one ignorant attains realization he is a saint. When a saint begins to understand he is ignorant.

> *It is better to realize mind than body.*
> *When mind is realized one need not worry*
>     *about body.*
> *When mind and body become one*
> *The man is free. Then he desires no praising.*

 ## 10. Seizei Alone & Poor

A MONK NAMED Seizei asked of Sozan: "Seizei is alone and poor. Will you give him support?"

Sozan asked: "Seizei?"

Seizei responded: "Yes, sir."

Sozan said: "You have Zen, the best wine in China, and already have finished three cups, and still you are saying that they did not even wet your lips."

*Mumon's comment:* Seizei overplayed his hand. Why was it so? Because Sozan had eyes and knew with whom to deal. Even so, I want to ask: At what point did Seizei drink wine?

> *The poorest man in China,*
> *The bravest man in China,*
> *He barely sustains himself,*
> *Yet wishes to rival the wealthiest.*

想
忘 11. *Joshu Examines a Monk in Meditation*

JOSHU WENT to a place where a monk had retired to meditate and asked him: "What is, is what?"

The monk raised his fist.

Joshu replied: "Ships cannot remain where the water is too shallow." And he left.

A few days later Joshu went again to visit the monk and asked the same question.

The monk answered the same way.

Joshu said: "Well given, well taken, well killed, well saved." And he bowed to the monk.

*Mumon's comment:* The raised fist was the same both times. Why is it Joshu did not admit the first and approved the second one? Where is the fault?

Whoever answers this knows that Joshu's tongue has no bone so he can use it freely. Yet perhaps Joshu is wrong. Or, through that monk, he may have discovered his mistake.

If anyone thinks that the one's insight exceeds the other's, he has no eyes.

> *The light of the eyes is as a comet,*
> *And Zen's activity is as lightning.*
> *The sword that kills the man*
> *Is the sword that saves the man.*

# 誤 12. Zuigan Calls His Own Master

ZUIGAN CALLED out to himself every day: "Master."
Then he answered himself: "Yes, sir."
And after that he added: "Become sober."
Again he answered: "Yes, sir."
"And after that," he continued, "do not be deceived by others."
"Yes, sir, yes, sir," he answered.

*Mumon's comment:* Old Zuigan sells out and buys himself. He is opening a puppet show. He uses one mask to call "Master" and another that answers the master. Another mask says "Sober up" and another, "Do not be cheated by others." If anyone clings to any of his masks, he is mistaken, yet if he imitates Zuigan, he will make himself fox-like.

> Some Zen students do not realize the true
>     man in a mask
> Because they recognize ego-soul.
> "Ego-soul is the seed of birth and death,
> And foolish people call it the true man.

# 椀 13. *Tokusan Holds His Bowl*

TOKUSAN WENT to the dining room from the meditation hall holding his bowl. Seppo was on duty cooking. When he met Tokusan he said: "The dinner drum is not yet beaten. Where are you going with your bowl?"

So Tokusan returned to his room.

Seppo told Ganto about this. Ganto said: "Old Tokusan did not understand ultimate truth."

Tokusan heard of this remark and asked Ganto to come to him. "I have heard," he said, "you are not approving my Zen." Ganto admitted this indirectly. Tokusan said nothing.

The next day Tokusan delivered an entirely different kind of lecture to the monks. Ganto laughed and clapped his hands, saying: "I see our old man understands ultimate truth indeed. None in China can surpass him."

*Mumon's comment:* Speaking about ultimate truth, both Ganto and Tokusan did not even dream it. After all, they are dummies.

> *Whoever understands the first truth*
> *Should understand the ultimate truth.*
> *The last and first,*
> *Are they not the same?*

# 斷 14. *Nansen Cuts the Cat in Two*

NANSEN SAW the monks of the eastern and western halls fighting over a cat. He seized the cat and told the monks: "If any of you say a good word, you can save the cat."

No one answered. So Nansen boldly cut the cat in two pieces.

That evening Joshu returned and Nansen told him about this. Joshu removed his sandals and, placing them on his head, walked out.

Nansen said: "If you had been there, you could have saved the cat."

*Mumon's comment:* Why did Joshu put his sandals on his head? If anyone answers this question, he will understand exactly how Nansen enforced the edict. If not, he should watch his own head.

> *Had Joshu been there,*
> *He would have enforced the edict oppositely.*
> *Joshu snatches the sword*
> *And Nansen begs for his life.*

質 *15. Tozan's Three Blows*

TOZAN WENT to Ummon. Ummon asked him where he had come from.

Tozan said: "From Sato village."

Ummon asked: "In what temple did you remain for the summer?"

Tozan replied: "The temple of Hoji, south of the lake."

"When did you leave there?" asked Ummon, wondering how long Tozan would continue with such factual answers.

"The twenty-fifth of August," answered Tozan.

Ummon said: "I should give you three blows with a stick, but today I forgive you."

The next day Tozan bowed to Ummon and asked: "Yesterday you forgave me three blows. I do not know why you thought me wrong."

Ummon, rebuking Tozan's spiritless responses, said: "You are good for nothing. You simply wander from one monastery to another."

Before Ummon's words were ended Tozan was enlightened.

*Mumon's comment:* Ummon fed Tozan good Zen food. If Tozan can digest it, Ummon may add another member to his family.

In the evening Tozan swam around in a sea of good and bad, but at dawn Ummon crushed his nutshell. After all, he wasn't so smart.

Now, I want to ask: Did Tozan deserve the three blows? If you say yes, not only Tozan but every one of you deserves them. If you say no, Ummon is speaking a lie. If you answer this question clearly, you can eat the same food as Tozan.

*The lioness teaches her cubs roughly;*
*The cubs jump and she knocks them down.*

> *When Ummon saw Tozan his first arrow*
> *was light;*
> *His second arrow shot deep.*

鍾 *16. Bells and Robes*

UMMON ASKED: "The world is such a wide world, why do you answer a bell and don ceremonial robes?"

*Mumon's comment:* When one studies Zen one need not follow sound or color or form. Even though some have attained insight when hearing a voice or seeing a color or a form, this is a very common way. It is not true Zen. The real Zen student controls sound, color, form, and actualizes the truth in his everyday life.

Sound comes to the ear, the ear goes to sound. When you blot out sound and sense, what do you understand? While listening with ears one never can understand. To understand intimately one should see sound.

> *When you understand, you belong to the family;*
> *When you do not understand, you are a stranger*
> *Those who do not understand belong to the family,*
> *And when they understand they are strangers.*

汲
答
*17. The Three Calls of
the Emperor's Teacher*

CHU, CALLED KOKUSHI, the teacher of the emperor, called to his attendant: "Oshin."

Oshin answered: "Yes."

Chu repeated, to test his pupil: "Oshin."

Oshin repeated: "Yes."

Chu called: "Oshin."

Oshin answered: "Yes."

Chu said: "I ought to apologize to you for all this calling, but really you ought to apologize to me."

*Mumon's comment:* When old Chu called Oshin three times his tongue was rotting, but when Oshin answered three times his words were brilliant. Chu was getting decrepit and lonesome, and his method of teaching was like holding a cow's head to feed it clover.

Oshin did not trouble to show his Zen either. His satisfied stomach had no desire to feast. When the country is prosperous everyone is indolent; when the home is wealthy the children are spoiled.

Now I want to ask you: Which one should apologize?

*When prison stocks are iron and have no place for the
head, the prisoner is doubly in trouble.*

*When there is no place for Zen in the head of our gener-
ation, it is in grievous trouble.*

*If you try to hold up the gate and door of a falling house,
You also will be in trouble.*

## 量 18. Toman's Three Pounds

A MONK ASKED Tozan when he was weighing
some flax: "What is Buddha?"

Tozan said: "This flax weighs three pounds."

*Mumon's comment:* Old Tozan's Zen is like a clam. The
minute the shell opens you see the whole inside. However, I want to ask you: Do you see the real Tozan?

> *Three pounds of flax in front of your nose,*
> *Close enough, and mind is still closer.*
> *Whoever talks about affirmation and negation*
> *Lives in the right and wrong region.*

常 *19. Everyday Life Is the Path*

JOSHU ASKED Nansen: "What is the path?'
Nansen said: "Everyday life is the path." Joshu asked:
"Can it be studied?"

Nansen said: "If you try to study, you will be far
away from it."

Joshu asked: "If I do not study, how can I know it
is the path?"

Nansen said: "The path does not belong to the perception world, neither does it belong to the nonper-
ception world. Cognition is a delusion and noncogni-
tion is senseless. If you want to reach the true path
beyond doubt, place yourself in the same freedom as
sky. You name it neither good nor not-good."

At these words Joshu was enlightened.

*Mumon's comment:* Nansen could melt Joshu's frozen
doubts at once when Joshu asked his questions. I
doubt though if Joshu reached the point that Nansen
did. He needed thirty more years of study.

> *In spring, hundreds of flowers; in autumn,*
>     *a harvest moon;*
> *In summer, a refreshing breeze; in winter,*
>     *snow will accompany you.*
> *If useless things do not hang in your mind,*
> *Any season is a good season for you.*

**鞋** *20. The Enlightened Man*

SHOGEN ASKED: "Why does the enlightened man not stand on his feet and explain himself?"

And he also said: "It is not necessary for speech to come from the tongue."

*Mumon's comment:* Shogen spoke plainly enough, but how many will understand? If anyone comprehends, he should come to my place and test out my big stick. Why, look here, to test real gold you must see it through fire.

> *If the feet of enlightenment moved, the great*
> *ocean would overflow;*
> *If that head bowed, it would look down upon*
> *the heavens.*
> *Such a body has no place to rest....*
> *Let another continue this poem.*

**塵** *21. Dried Dung*

A MONK ASKED Ummon: "What is Buddha?" Ummon answered him: "Dried dung."

*Mumon's comment:* It seems to me Ummon is so poor he cannot distinguish the taste of one food from another, or else he is too busy to write readable letters. Well, he tried to hold his school with dried dung. And his teaching was just as useless.

> *Lightning flashes,*
> *Sparks shower.*
> *In one blink of your eyes*
> *You have missed seeing.*

## 弟 22. Kashapa's Preaching Sign

ANANDA ASKED Kashapa: "Buddha gave you the golden-woven robe of successorship. What else did he give you?"

Kashapa said: "Ananda."

Ananda answered: "Yes, brother."

Said Kashapa: "Now you can take down my preaching sign and put up your own."

*Mumon's comment:* If one understands this, he will see the old brotherhood still gathering, but if not, even though he has studied the truth from ages before the Buddhas, he will not attain enlightenment.

*The point of the question is dull but the answer*
    *is intimate.*
*How many persons hearing it will open their eyes?*
*Elder brother calls and younger brother answers,*
*This spring does not belong to the ordinary season.*

不
考

## 23. Do Not Think Good, Do Not Think Not-Good

WHEN HE BECAME emancipated the sixth patriarch received from the fifth patriarch the bowl and
robe given from the Buddha to his successors, generation after generation.

A monk named E-myo out of envy pursued the
patriarch to take this great treasure away from him.
The sixth patriarch placed the bowl and robe on a
stone in the road and told E-myo: "These objects just
symbolize the faith. There is no use fighting over
them. If you desire to take them, take them now."

When E-myo went to move the bowl and robe they
were as heavy as mountains. He could not budge them.
Trembling for shame he said: " I came wanting the
teaching, not the material treasures. Please teach me."

The sixth patriarch said: "When you do not think
good and when you do not think not-good, what is
your true self?"

At these words E-myo was illumined. Perspiration broke out all over his body. He cried and bowed, saying: "You have given me the secret words and meanings. Is there yet a deeper part of the teaching?"

The sixth patriarch replied: "What I have told you is no secret at all. When you realize your own true self the secret belongs to you."

E-myo said: "I was under the fifth patriarch many years but could not realize my true self until now. Through your teaching I find the source. A person drinks water and knows himself whether it is cold or warm. May I call you my teacher?"

The sixth patriarch replied: "We studied together under the fifth patriarch. Call him your teacher, but just treasure what you have attained."

*Mumon's comment:* The sixth patriarch certainly was kind in such an emergency. It was as if he removed the skin and seeds from the fruit and then, opening the pupil's mouth, let him eat.

> *You cannot describe it, you cannot picture it,*
> *You cannot admire it, you cannot sense it.*
> *It is your true self it has nowhere to hide.*
> *When the world is destroyed, it will not be*
>     *destroyed.*

# 左 24. Without Words, Without Silence

A MONK ASKED Fuketsu: "Without speaking, without silence, how can you express the truth?" Fuketsu observed: "I always remember springtime in southern China. The birds sing among innumerable kinds of fragrant flowers."

*Mumon's comment:* Fuketsu used to have lightning Zen. Whenever he had the opportunity, he flashed it. But this time he failed to do so and only borrowed from an old Chinese poem. Never mind Fuketsu's Zen. If you want to express the truth, throw out your words, throw out your silence, and tell me about your own Zen.

> *Without revealing his own penetration,*
> *He offered another's words, not his to give.*
> *Had he chattered on and on,*
> *Even his listeners would have been embarrassed.*

浮 25. *Preaching from the Third Seat*

IN A DREAM Kyozan went to Maitreya's Pure Land. He recognized himself seated in the third seat in the abode of Maitreya. Someone announced: "Today the one who sits in the third seat will preach."

Kyozan arose and, hitting the gavel, said: "The truth of Mahayana teaching is transcendent, above words and thought. Do you understand?"

*Mumon's comment:* I want to ask you monks: Did he preach or did he not?

When he opens his mouth he is lost. When he seals his mouth he is lost. If he does not open it, if he does not seal it, he is 108,000 miles from truth.

> *In the light of day,*
> *Yet in a dream he talks of a dream.*
> *A monster among monsters,*
> *He intended to deceive the whole crowd.*

# 簾 26. Two Monks Roll Up the Screen

HOGEN OF SEIRYO monastery was about to lecture before dinner when he noticed that the bamboo screen lowered for meditation had not been rolled up. He pointed to it. Two monks arose from the audience and rolled it up.

Hogen, observing the physical moment, said: "The state of the first monk is good, not that of the other."

*Mumon's comment:* I want to ask you: Which of those two monks gained and which lost? If any of you has one eye, he will see the failure on the teacher's part. However, I am not discussing gain and loss.

> *When the screen is rolled up the great sky opens,*
> *Yet the sky is not attuned to Zen.*
> *It is best to forget the great sky*
> *And to retire from every wind.*

**唯**
**無**
## 27. It Is Not Mind, It Is Not Buddha, It Is Not Things

A MONK ASKED Nansen: "Is there a teaching no master ever preached before?"

Nansen said: "Yes, there is."

"What is it?" asked the monk.

Nansen replied: "It is not mind, it is not Buddha, it is not things."

*Mumon's comment:* Old Nansen gave away his treasure-words. He must have been greatly upset.

> *Nansen was too kind and lost his treasure.*
> *Truly, words have no power.*
> *Even though the mountain becomes the sea,*
> *Words cannot open another's mind.*

**灰**
## 28. Blow Out the Candle

TOKUSAN WAS studying Zen under Ryutan. One night he came to Ryutan and asked many questions. The teacher said: "The night is getting old. Why don't you retire?"

So Tokusan bowed and opened the screen to go out, observing: "It is very dark outside."

Ryutan offered Tokusan a lighted candle to find his way. Just as Tokusan received it, Ryutan blew it out. At that moment the mind of Tokusan was opened.

"What have you attained?" asked Ruytan.

"From now on," said Tokusan, "I will not doubt the teacher's words."

The next day Ryutan told the monks at his lecture: "I see one monk among you. His teeth are like the sword tree, his mouth is like the blood bowl. If you hit him hard with a big stick, he will not even so much as look back at you. Someday he will mount the highest peak and carry my teaching there."

On that day, in front of the lecture hall, Tokusan burned to ashes his commentaries on the sutras. He said: "However abstruse the teachings are, in comparison with this enlightenment they are like a single hair to the great sky. However profound the complicated knowledge of the world, compared to this enlightenment it is like one drop of water to the great ocean." Then he left that monastery.

*Mumon's comment:* When Tokusan was in his own country he was not satisfied with Zen although he had heard about it. He thought: "Those Southern monks say they can teach Dharma outside of the sutras. They are all wrong. I must teach them." So he traveled south. He happened to stop near Ryutan's monastery for refreshments. An old woman who was there asked him: "What are you carrying so heavily?"

Tokusan replied: "This is a commentary I have made on the Diamond Sutra after many years of work."

The old woman said: "I read that sutra which says: 'The past mind cannot be held, the present mind cannot be held, the future mind cannot be held.' You wish some tea and refreshments. Which mind do you propose to use for them?"

Tokusan was as though dumb. Finally he asked the woman: "Do you know of any good teacher around here?"

The old woman referred him to Ryutan, not more than five miles away. So he went to Ryutan in all humility, quite different from when he had started his journey. Ryutan in turn was so kind he forgot his own dignity. It was like pouring muddy water over a drunken man to sober him. After all, it was an unnecessary comedy.

> *A hundred hearings cannot surpass one seeing,*
> *But after you see the teacher, that one glance*
> *cannot surpass a hundred hearings.*
> *His nose was very high*
> *But he was blind after all.*

探 *29. Not the Wind, Not the Flag*

TWO MONKS were arguing about a flag. One said: "The flag is moving." The other said: "The wind is moving."

The sixth patriarch happened to be passing by. He told them: "Not the wind, not the flag; mind is moving."

*Mumon's comment:* The sixth patriarch said: "The wind is not moving, the flag is not moving. Mind is moving." What did he mean? If you understand this intimately, you will see the two monks there trying to buy iron and gaining gold. The sixth patriarch could not bear to see those two dull heads, so he made such a bargain.

> *Wind, flag, mind moves,*
> *The same understanding.*
> *When the mouth opens*
> *All are wrong.*

精 *30. This Mind Is Buddha*

DAIBAI ASKED Baso: "What is Buddha?" Baso said: "This mind is Buddha."

*Mumon's comment:* If anyone wholly understands this, he is wearing Buddha's clothing, he is eating Buddha's food, he is speaking Buddha's words, he is behaving as Buddha, he is Buddha.

This anecdote, however, has given many a pupil the sickness of formality. If one truly understands, he will wash out his mouth for three days after saying the word Buddha, and he will close his ears and flee after hearing "This mind is Buddha."

> *Under blue sky, in bright sunlight,*
> *One need not search around.*
> *Asking what Buddha is*
> *Is like hiding loot in one's pocket and declaring*
> *      oneself innocent.*

# 探 31. Joshu Investigates

A TRAVELING MONK asked an old woman the road to Taizan, a popular temple supposed to give wisdom to the one who worships there. The old woman said: "Go straight ahead." When the monk proceeded a few steps, she said to herself: "He also is a common church-goer."

Someone told this incident to Joshu, who said: "Wait until I investigate." The next day he went and asked the same question, and the old woman gave the same answer.

Joshu remarked: "I have investigated that old woman."

*Mumon's comment:* The old woman understood how war is planned, but she did not know how spies sneak in behind her tent. Old Joshu played the spy's work and turned the tables on her, but he was not an able general. Both had their faults. Now I want to ask you: What was the point of Joshu's investigating the old woman?

> *When the question is common*
> *The answer is also common.*
> *When the question is sand in a bowl of*
> *     boiled rice*
> *The answer is a stick in the soft mud.*

# 哲 32. A Philosopher Asks Buddha

A PHILOSOPHER ASKED Buddha: "Without words, without the wordless, will you tell me truth?"

The Buddha kept silence.

The philosopher bowed and thanked the Buddha, saying: "With your loving kindness I have cleared away my delusions and entered the true path."

After the philosopher had gone, Ananda asked the Buddha what he had attained.

The Buddha replied: "A good horse runs even at the shadow of the whip."

*Mumon's comment:* Ananda was the disciple of the Buddha. Even so, his opinion did not surpass that of outsiders. I want to ask you monks: How much difference is there between disciples and outsiders?

> *To tread the sharp edge of a sword,*
> *To run on smooth-frozen ice,*
> *One needs no footsteps to follow.*
> *Walk over the cliffs with hands free.*

**粋** *33. This Mind Is Not Buddha*

A MONK ASKED Baso: "What is Buddha?" Baso said: "This mind is not Buddha."

*Mumon's comment:* If anyone understands this, he is a graduate of Zen.

> *If you meet a fencing-master on the road, you*
>     *may give him your sword,*
> *If you meet a poet, you may offer him your poem.*
> *When you meet others, say only a part of what*
>     *you intend.*
> *Never give the whole thing at once.*

**羞** *34. Learning Is Not the Path*

NANSEN SAID: "Mind is not Buddha. Learning is not the path."

*Mumon's comment:* Nansen was getting old and forgot to be ashamed. He spoke out with bad breath and exposed the scandal of his own home.

However, there are few who appreciate his kindness.

*When the sky is clear the sun appears,*
*When the earth is parched rain will fall.*
*He opened his heart fully and spoke out,*
*But it was useless to talk to pigs and fish.*

## 双 35. *Two Souls*

"SEIJO, THE CHINESE girl," observed Goso, "had two souls, one always sick at home and the other in the city, a married woman with two children. Which was the true soul?"

*Mumon's comment:* When one understands this, he will know it is possible to come out from one shell and enter another, as if one were stopping at a transient lodging house. But if he cannot understand, when his time comes and his four elements separate, he will be just like a crab dipped in boiling water, struggling with many hands and legs. In such a predicament he may say: "Mumon did not tell me where to go!" but it will be too late then.

*The moon above the clouds is the same moon,*
*The mountains and rivers below are all different.*
*Each is happy in its unity and variety.*
*This is one, this is two.*

## 36. Meeting a Zen Master on the Road

GOSO SAID: "When you meet a Zen master on the road you cannot talk to him, you cannot face him with silence. What are you going to do?"

*Mumon's comment:* In such a case, if you can answer him intimately, your realization will be beautiful, but if you cannot, you should look about without seeing anything.

> *Meeting a Zen master on the road,*
> *Face him neither with words nor silence.*
> *Give him an uppercut*
> *And you will be called one who understands Zen.*

## 37. A Buffalo Passes Through the Enclosure

GOSO SAID: "When a buffalo goes out of his enclosure to the edge of the abyss, his horns and his head and his hoofs all pass through, but why can't the tail also pass?"

*Mumon's comment:* If anyone can open one eye at this point and say a word of Zen, he is qualified to repay the four gratifications, and, not only that, he can save all sentient beings under him. But if he cannot say such a word of true Zen, he should turn back to his tail.

> *If the buffalo runs, he will fall into the trench;*
> *If he returns, he will be butchered.*
> *That little tail*
> *Is a very strange thing.*

# 樫 38. An Oak Tree in the Garden

A MONK ASKED Joshu why Bodhidharma came to China. Joshu said: "An oak tree in the garden."

*Mumon's comment:* If one sees Joshu's answer clearly, there is no Shakyamuni Buddha before him and no future Buddha after him.

> *Words cannot describe everything.*
> *The heart's message cannot be delivered in words.*
> *If one receives words literally, he will be lost,*
> *If he tries to explain with words, he will not*
>     *attain enlightenment in this life.*

# 欸 39. Ummon's Sidetrack

A ZEN STUDENT told Ummon: "Brilliancy of Buddha illuminates the whole universe."

Before he finished the phrase Ummon asked: "You are reciting another's poem, are you not?"

"Yes," answered the student.

"You are sidetracked," said Ummon.

Afterwards another teacher, Shishin, asked his pupils: "At what point did that student go off the track?"

*Mumon's comment:* If anyone perceives Ummon's particular skillfulness, he will know at what point the student was off the track, and he will be a teacher of man and Devas. If not, he cannot even perceive himself.

> *When a fish meets the fishhook*
> *If he is too greedy, he will be caught.*
> *When his month opens*
> *His life already is lost.*

壷 *40. Tipping Over a Water Vase*

HYAKUJO WISHED to send a monk to open a new monastery. He told his pupils that whoever answered a question most ably would be appointed. Placing a water vase on the ground, he asked: "Who can say what this is without calling its name?"

The chief monk said: "No one can call it a wooden shoe."

Isan, the cooking monk, tipped over the vase with his foot and went out.

Hyakujo smiled and said: "The chief monk loses." And Isan became the master of the new monastery.

*Mumon's comment:* Isan was brave enough, but he could not escape Hyakujo's trick. After all, he gave up a light job and took a heavy one. Why, can't you see, he took off his comfortable hat and placed himself in iron stocks.

> *Giving up cooking utensils,*
> *Defeating the chatterbox,*
> *Though his teacher sets a barrier*
>     *for him*
> *His feet will tip over everything,*
>     *even the Buddha.*

壁 *41. Bodhidharma Pacifies the Mind*

BODHIDHARMA SITS facing the wall. His future successor stands in the snow and presents his severed arm to Bodhidharma. He cries: "My mind is not pacified. Master, pacify my mind."

Bodhidharma says: "If you bring me that mind, I will pacify it for you."

The successor says: "When I search my mind I cannot hold it."

Bodhidharma says: "Then your mind is pacified already."

*Mumon's comment:* That broken-toothed old Hindu, Bodhidharma, came thousands of miles over the sea from India to China as if he had something wonderful. He is like raising waves without wind. After he remained years in China he had only one disciple and that one lost his arm and was deformed. Alas, ever since he has had brainless disciples.

> *Why did Bodhidharma come to China?*
> *For years monks have discussed this.*
> *All the troubles that have followed since*
> *Came from that teacher and disciple.*

生
起 *42. The Girl Comes Out from Meditation*

IN THE TIME of Buddha Shakyamuni, Manjusri went to the assemblage of the Buddhas. When he arrived there, the conference was over and each Buddha had returned to his own Buddha-land. Only one girl was yet unmoved in deep meditation.

Manjusri asked Buddha Shakyamuni how it was possible for this girl to reach this state, one which even he could not attain. "Bring her out from Samadhi and ask her yourself," said the Buddha.

Manjusri walked around the girl three times and snapped his fingers. She still remained in meditation. So by his miracle power he transported her to a high heaven and tried his best to call her, but in vain.

Buddha Shakyamuni said: "Even a hundred thousand Manjusris could not disturb her, but below this place, past twelve hundred million countries, is a Bodhisattva, Mo-myo, seed of delusion. If he comes here, she will awaken."

No sooner had the Buddha spoken than that Bodhisattva sprang up from the earth and bowed and paid homage to the Buddha. Buddha directed him to arouse the girl. The Bodhisattva went in front of the girl and snapped his fingers, and in that instant the girl came out from her deep meditation.

*Mumon's comment:* Old Shakyamuni set a very poor stage. I want to ask you monks: If Manjusri, who is supposed to have been the teacher of seven Buddhas, could not bring this girl out of meditation, how then could a Bodhisattva who was a mere beginner?

If you understand this intimately, you yourself can enter the great meditation while you are living in the world of delusion.

> *One could not awaken her, the other could.*
> *Neither are good actors.*
> *One wears the mask of god, one a devil's mask.*
> *Had both failed, the drama still would be*
>     *a comedy.*

# 短 43. Shuzan's Short Staff

SHUZAN HELD OUT his short staff and said: "If you call this a short staff, you oppose its reality. If you do not call it a short staff, you ignore the fact. Now what do you wish to call this?"

*Mumon's comment:* If you call this a short staff, you oppose its reality. If you do not call it a short staff, you ignore the fact. It cannot be expressed with words and it cannot be expressed without words. Now say quickly what it is.

*Holding out the short staff,*
*He gave an order of life or death.*
*Positive and negative interwoven,*
*Even Buddhas and patriarchs cannot*
    *escape this attack.*

# 杖 44. Basho's Staff

BASHO SAID to his disciple: "When you have a staff, I will give it to you. If you have no staff, I will take it away from you."

*Mumon's comment:* When there is no bridge over the creek the staff will help me. When I return home on a moonless night the staff will accompany me. But if you call this a staff, you will enter hell like an arrow.

*With this staff in my hand*
*I can measure the depths and shallows*
    *of the world.*
*The staff supports the heavens and makes*
    *firm the earth.*
*Everywhere it goes the true teaching*
    *will be spread.*

# 誰 45. Who Is He?

HOEN SAID: "The past and future Buddhas, both are his servants. Who is he?"

*Mumon's comment:* If you realize clearly who he is, it is as if you met your own father on a busy street. There is no need to ask anyone whether or not your recognition is true.

> *Do not fight with another's bow and arrow.*
> *Do not ride another's horse.*
> *Do not discuss another's faults.*
> *Do not interfere with another's work.*

# 飛昇 46. Proceed from the Top of the Pole

SEKISO ASKED: "How can you proceed on from the top of a hundred-foot pole?" Another Zen teacher said: "One who sits on the top of a hundred-foot pole has attained a certain height but still is not handling Zen freely. He should proceed on from there and appear with his whole body in the ten parts of the world."

*Mumon's comment:* One can continue his steps or turn his body freely about on the top of the pole. In either case he should be respected. I want to ask you monks, however: How will you proceed from the top of that pole? Look out!

> *The man who lacks the third eye of insight*
> *Will cling to the measure of the hundred feet.*
> *Such a man will jump from there and kill*
>     *himself,*
> *Like a blind man misleading other blind men.*

關 *47. Three Gates of Tosotsu*

TOSOTSU BUILT three barriers and made the monks pass through them. The first barrier is studying Zen. In studying Zen the aim is to see one's own true nature. Now where is your true nature?

Secondly, when one realizes his own true nature he will be free from birth and death. Now when you shut the light from your eyes and become a corpse, how can you free yourself?

Thirdly, if you free yourself from birth and death, you should know where you are. Now your body separates into the four elements. Where are you?

*Mumon's comment:* Whoever can pass these three barriers will be a master wherever he stands. Whatever happens about him he will turn into Zen.

Otherwise he will be living on poor food and not even enough of that to satisfy himself.

> *An instant realization sees endless time.*
> *Endless time is as one moment.*
> *When one comprehends the endless moment*
> *He realizes the person who is seeing it.*

# 附 *48. One Road of Kembo*

A ZEN PUPIL asked Kembo: "All Buddhas of the ten parts of the universe enter the one road of Nirvana. Where does that road begin?"

Kembo, raising his walking stick and drawing the figure one in the air, said: "Here it is."

This pupil went to Ummon and asked the same question. Ummon, who happened to have a fan in his hand, said: "This fan will reach to the thirty-third heaven and hit the nose of the presiding deity there. It is like the Dragon Carp of the Eastern Sea tipping over the rain-cloud with his tail."

*Mumon's comment:* One teacher enters the deep sea and scratches the earth and raises dust. The other goes to the mountaintop and raises waves that almost touch heaven. One holds, the other gives out. Each supports the profound teaching with a single hand. Kembo and Ummon are like two riders neither of whom can surpass the other. It is very difficult to find the perfect man. Frankly, neither of them know where the road starts.

> *Before the first step is taken the goal is reached.*
> *Before the tongue is moved the speech is finished.*
> *More than brilliant intuition is needed*
> *To find the origin of the right road.*

## 附 49. Amban's Addition

AMBAN, A LAYMAN Zen student, said: "Mu-mon has just published forty-eight koans and called the book *Gateless Gate*. He criticizes the old patriarchs' words and actions. I think he is very mischievous. He is like an old doughnut seller trying to catch a passer-by to force his doughnuts down his mouth. The customer can neither swallow nor spit out the doughnuts, and this causes suffering. Mu-mon has annoyed everyone enough, so I think I shall add one more as a bargain. I wonder if he himself can eat this bargain. If he can, and digest it well, it will be fine, but if not, we will have to put it back into the frying pan with his forty-eight also and cook them again. Mumon, you eat first, before someone else does:

"Buddha, according to a sutra, once said: 'Stop, stop. Do not speak. The ultimate truth is not even to think.'"

*Amban's comment:* Where did that so-called teaching come from? How is it that one could not even think it? Suppose someone spoke about it then what became of it? Buddha himself was a great chatterbox and in this sutra spoke contrarily. Because of this, persons like Mu-mon appear afterwards in China and make useless doughnuts, annoying people. What shall we do after all? I will show you. Then Amban put his palms together, folded his hands, and said: "Stop, stop. Do not speak. The ultimate truth is not even to think. And now I will make a little circle on the sutra with my finger and add that five thousand other sutras and Vimalakirti's gateless gate all are here!"

> *If anyone tells you fire is light,*
> *Pay no attention.*
> *When two thieves meet they need no*
> *introduction:*
> *They recognize each other without question.*

# 10 BULLS

by Kakuan
Illustrated by Tomikichiro Tokuriki

*Transcribed by Nyogen Senzaki and Paul Reps*

The enlightenment for which Zen aims, for which Zen exists, comes of itself. As consciousness, one moment it does not exist, the next it does. But physical man walks in the element of time even as he walks in mud, dragging his feet and his true nature.

So even Zen must compromise and recognize progressive steps of awareness leading closer to the ever instant of enlightenment.

That is what this book is about. In the twelfth century the Chinese master Kakuan drew the pictures of the ten bulls, basing them on earlier Taoist bulls, and wrote the comments in prose and verse translated here. His version was pure Zen, going deeper than earlier versions, which had ended with the nothingness of the eighth picture. It has been a constant source of inspiration to students ever since, and many illustrations of Kakuan's bulls have been made through the centuries.

The illustrations reproduced here are modern versions by the noted Kyoto woodblock artist Tomikichiro Tokuriki, descendant of a long line of artists and proprietor of the Daruma-do teashop (Daruma is the Japanese name for Bod-

*hidharma, the first Zen patriarch). His oxherding pictures are as delightfully direct and timelessly meaningful as Kakuan's original pictures must have been.*

*The following is adapted from the preface by Nyogen Senzaki and Paul Reps to the first edition of their translation.*

*The bull is the eternal principle of life, truth in action. The ten bulls represent sequent steps in the realization of one's true nature.*

*This sequence is as potent today as it was when Kakuan (1100-1200) developed it from earlier works and made his paintings of the bull. Here in America we perform a similar work eight centuries later to keep the bull invigorated. (There in Kyoto, Tokuriki has done the same)*

*An understanding of the creative principle transcends any time or place. The 10 Bulls is more than poetry, more than pictures. It is a revelation of spiritual unfoldment paralleled in every bible of human experience. May the reader, like the Chinese patriarch, discover the footprints of his potential self and, carrying the staff of his purpose and the wine jug of his true desire, frequent the market place and there enlighten others.*

## 1. The Search for the Bull

*In the pasture of this world, I endlessly push*
*aside the tall grasses in search of the bull.*
*Following unnamed rivers, lost upon the*
*interpenetrating paths of distant mountains,*
*My strength failing and my vitality exhausted,*
*I cannot find the bull.*
*I only hear the locusts chirring through the*
*forest at night.*

*Comment:* The bull never has been lost. What need is there to search? Only because of separation from my true nature, I fail to find him. In the confusion of the senses I lose even his tracks. Far from home, I see many crossroads, but which way is the right one I know not. Greed and fear, good and bad, entangle me.

一
尋牛

## 2. Discovering the Footprints

*Along the riverbank under the trees, I discover*
*footprints!*
*Even under the fragrant grass I see his prints.*
*Deep in remote mountains they are found.*
*These traces no more can be hidden than one's*
*nose, looking heavenward.*

*Comment:* Understanding the teaching, I see the footprints of the bull. Then I learn that, just as many utensils are made from one metal, so too are myriad entities made of the fabric of self. Unless I discriminate, how will I perceive the true from the untrue? Not yet having entered the gate, nevertheless I have discerned the path.

## 3. Perceiving the Bull

*I hear the song of the nightingale.*
*The sun is warm, the wind is mild, willows*
*    are green along the shore,*
*Here no bull can hide!*
*What artist can draw that massive head,*
*    those majestic horns?*

*Comment:* When one hears the voice, one can sense its source. As soon as the six senses merge, the gate is entered. Wherever one enters one sees the head of the bull! This unity is like salt in water, like color in dye-stuff. The slightest thing is not apart from self.

見牛
三

## 4. Catching the Bull

*I seize him with a terrific struggle.*
*His great will and power are inexhaustible.*
*He charges to the high plateau far above the*
*cloud-mists,*
*Or in an impenetrable ravine he stands.*

*Comment:* He dwelt in the forest a long time, but I caught him today! Infatuation for scenery interferes with his direction. Longing for sweeter grass, he wanders away. His mind still is stubborn and unbridled. If I wish him to submit, I must raise my whip.

## 5. Taming the Bull

*The whip and rope are necessary,*
*Else he might stray off down some dusty road.*
*Being well trained, he becomes naturally*
  *gentle.*
*Then, unfettered, he obeys his master.*

*Comment:* When one thought arises, another thought follows. When the first thought springs from enlightenment, all subsequent thoughts are true. Through delusion, one makes everything untrue. Delusion is not caused by objectivity; it is the result of subjectivity. Hold the nose-ring tight and do not allow even a doubt.

五
牧牛

## 6. Riding the Bull Home

*Mounting the bull, slowly I return homeward.*
*The voice of my flute intones through the*
*evening.*
*Measuring with hand-beats the pulsating*
*harmony, I direct the endless rhythm.*
*Whoever hears this melody will join me.*

*Comment:* This struggle is over; gain and loss are assimilated. I sing the song of the village woodsman, and play the tunes of the children. Astride the bull, I observe the clouds above. Onward I go, no matter who may wish to call me back.

六騎牛歸來

## 7. The Bull Transcended

*Astride the bull, I reach home.*
*I am serene. The bull too can rest.*
*The dawn has come. In blissful repose,*
*Within my thatched dwelling I have abandoned*
*    the whip and rope.*

*Comment:* All is one law, not two. We only make the
bull a temporary subject. It is as the relation of rabbit
and trap, of fish and net. It is as gold and dross, or the
moon emerging from a cloud. One path of clear light
travels on throughout endless time.

七　忘牛存人

## 8. Both Bull & Self Transcended

*Whip, rope, person, and bull—all merge in*
*    No -Thing.*
*This heaven is so vast no message can stain it.*
*How may a snowflake exist in a raging fire?*
*Here are the footprints of the patriarchs.*

*Comment:* Mediocrity is gone. Mind is clear of limita-
tion. I seek no state of enlightenment. Neither do I
remain where no enlightenment exists. Since I linger
in neither condition, eyes cannot see me. If hundreds
of birds strew my path with flowers, such praise
would be meaningless.

八
人牛
俱
忘

## 9. Reaching the Source

*Too many steps have been taken returning to*
*   the root and the source.*
*Better to have been blind and deaf from the*
*   beginning!*
*Dwelling in one's true abode, unconcerned*
*   with that without—*
*The river flows tranquilly on and the flowers*
*   are red.*

*Comment:* From the beginning, truth is clear. Poised in silence, I observe the forms of integration and disintegration. One who is not attached to "form" need not be "reformed." The water is emerald, the mountain is indigo, and I see that which is creating and that which is destroying.

返本
還源

## 10. In the World

*Barefooted and naked of breast, I mingle with*
*the people of the world.*
*My clothes are ragged and dust-laden, and*
*I am ever blissful.*
*I use no magic to extend my life;*
*Now, before me, the dead trees become alive.*

*Comment:* Inside my gate, a thousand sages do not know me. The beauty of my garden is invisible. Why should one search for the footprints of the patriarchs? I go to the market place with my wine bottle and return home with my staff. I visit the wineshop and the market, and everyone I look upon becomes enlightened.

十
入鄽
垂手

昭和辛卯夏
富吉郎
画並刻摺

# CENTERING

*Transcribed by Paul Reps*

*Zen is nothing new, neither is it anything old. Long before Buddha was born the search was on in India, as the present work shows.*

*Long after man has forgotten such words as Zen and Buddha, satori and koan, China and Japan and America — still the search will go on, still Zen will be seen even in flowers and grass-blades before the sun.*

*The following is adapted from the preface to the first version in English of this ancient work.*

*Wandering in the ineffable beauty of Kashmir, above Srinagar I come upon the hermitage of Lakshmanjoo.*

*It overlooks green rice fields, the gardens of Shalimar and Nishat Bagh, lakes fringed with lotus. Water streams down from a mountaintop.*

*Here Lakshmanjoo—tall, full-bodied, shining—welcomes me. He shares with me this ancient teaching from the Vigyan Bhairava and Sochanda Tantra, both written about four thousand years ago, and from Malini Vijaya Tantra, probably another thousand years older yet. It is an ancient teaching, copied and recopied countless times, and from it*

*Lakshmanjoo has made the beginnings of an English ver-*
*sion. I transcribe it eleven more times to get it into the form*
*given here.*

*Shiva first chanted it to his consort Devi in a language*
*of love we have yet to learn. It is about the immanent expe-*
*rience. It presents 112 ways to open the invisible door of*
*consciousness. I see Lakshmanjoo gives his life to its prac-*
*ticing.*

*Some of the ways may appear redundant, yet each dif-*
*fers from any other. Some may seem simple, yet any one*
*requires constant dedication even to test it.*

*Machines, ledgers, dancers, athletes balance. Just as*
*centering or balance augments various skills, so it may*
*awareness. As an experiment, try standing equally on both*
*feet; then imagine you are shifting your balance slightly*
*from foot to foot: just as balance centers, do you.*

*If we are conscious in part, this implies more inclusive*
*consciousness. Have you a hand? Yes. That you know with-*
*out doubt. But until asked the question were you cognizant*
*of the hand apart?*

*Surely men as inspirators, known and unknown to the*
*world, have shared a common uncommon discovery. The*
*Tao of Lao-tse, Nirvana of Buddha, Jehovah of Moses, the*
*Father of Jesus, the Allah of Mohammed— all point to the*
*experience.*

*No-thing-ness, spirit—once touched, the whole life*
*clears.*

DEVI SAYS:

O Shiva, what is your reality?
What is this wonder-filled universe?
What constitutes seed?
Who centers the universal wheel?
What is this life beyond form pervading forms?
How may we enter it fully, above space and time, names and descriptions?
Let my doubts be cleared!

SHIVA REPLIES:

*(Devi, though already enlightened, has asked the foregoing questions so others through the universe might receive Shiva's instructions. Now follow Shiva's reply, giving the 112 ways.)*

1. Radiant one, this experience may dawn between two breaths. After breath comes in (down) and just before turning up (out)—*the beneficence.*

2. As breath turns from down to up, and again as breath curves from up to down—through both these turns, *realize*.

3. Or, whenever inbreath and outbreath fuse, at this instant touch the energyless energy-filled *center*.

4. Or, when breath is all out (up) and stopped of itself, or all in (down) and stopped—in such universal pause, one's small self *vanishes*. This is difficult only for the impure.

5. Consider your essence as light rays rising from center to center up the vertebrae, and so rises *livingness* in you.

6. Or in the spaces between, feel this as *lightning*.

7. Devi, imagine the Sanskrit letters in these honey-filled foci of awareness, first as letters, then more subtly as sounds, then as most subtle feeling. Then, leaving them aside, be *free*.

8. Attention between eyebrows, let mind be before thought. Let form fill with breath-essence to the top of the head, and there *shower as light*.

9. Or, imagine the five-colored circles of the peacock tail to be your five senses in illimitable space. Now let their beauty melt within. Similarly, at any point in space or on a wall—until the point *dissolves*. Then your wish for another comes true.

10. Eyes closed, see your inner being in detail. Thus *see* your true nature.

11. Place your whole attention in the nerve, delicate as the lotus thread, in the center of your spinal column. In such *be transformed*.

12. Closing the seven openings of the head with your hands, a space between your eyes becomes *all-inclusive*.

13. Touching eyeballs as a feather, lightness between them *opens into heart* and there permeates the cosmos.

14. Bathe in the center of sound, as in the continuous sound of a waterfall. Or, by putting fingers in ears, hear *the sound of sounds*.

15. Intone a sound, as *a-u-m*, slowly. As sound enters soundfulness, *so do you*.

16. In the beginning and gradual refinement of the sound of any letter, *awake*.

17. While listening to stringed instruments, hear their composite central sound; thus *omnipresence*.

18. Intone a sound audibly, then less and less audibly as feeling deepens into *this silent harmony*.

19. Imagine spirit simultaneously within and around you until the entire universe *spiritualizes*.

20. Kind Devi, enter etheric *presence* pervading far above and below your form.

21. Put mindstuff in such inexpressible fineness above, below, and *in your heart*.

22. Consider any area of your present form as *limitlessly spacious*.

23. Feel your substance, bones, flesh, blood, saturated with *cosmic essence*.

24. Suppose your passive form to be an empty room with walls of skin—*empty*.

25. Blessed one, as senses are absorbed in heart, reach the *center* of the lotus.

26. Unminding mind, keep in the middle—*until*.

27. When in worldly activity, keep attentive between the two breaths, and so practicing, in a few days *be born anew*. (Lakshmanjoo says this is his favorite.)

28. Focus on fire rising through your form from the toes up until the body burns to ashes *but not you*.

29. Meditate on the make-believe world as burning to ashes, and become *being above human*.

30. Feel the fine qualities of creativity permeating your breasts and assuming *delicate configurations*.

31. With intangible breath in center of forehead, as this reaches heart at the moment of sleep, have direction over dreams and *over death itself*.

32. As, subjectively, letters flow into words and words into sentences, and as, objectively, circles flow into worlds and worlds into principles, find at last these converging *in our being*.

33. Gracious one, play the universe is an empty shell wherein your mind frolics *infinitely*.

34. Look upon a bowl without seeing the sides or the material. In a few moments *become aware*.

35. Abide in some place *endlessly spacious*, clear of trees, hills, habitations. Thence comes the end of mind pressures.

36. Sweet-hearted one, meditate on knowing and not knowing, existing and not existing. Then leave both aside that you may *be*.

37. Look lovingly on some object. Do not go on to another object. Here, in the middle of this object—*the blessing*.

38. Feel cosmos as *translucent ever-living presence*.

39. With utmost devotion, center on the two junctions of breath and know the *knower*.

40. Consider the plenum to be your own *body of bliss*.

41. While being caressed, sweet princess, enter *the caressing* as everlasting life.

42. Stop the doors of senses when feeling the creeping of an ant. *Then*.

43. At the start of sexual union, keep attentive on the fire *in the beginning*, and, so continuing, avoid the embers in the end.

44. When in such embrace your senses are shaken as leaves, *enter this shaking*.

45. Even remembering union, without the embrace, *the transformation*.

46. On joyously seeing a long-absent friend, *permeate this joy*.

47. When eating or drinking, become the taste of the food or drink, and *be filled*.

48. O lotus-eyed one, sweet of touch, when singing, seeing, tasting, be aware you are and discover *the everliving*.

49. Wherever satisfaction is found, in whatever act, *actualize this*.

50. At the point of sleep when sleep has not yet come and external wakefulness vanishes, at this point *being* is revealed. (Lakshmanjoo says this is another of his favorites.)

51. In summer when you see the entire sky endlessly clear, *enter such clarity.*

52. Lie down as dead. Enraged in wrath, stay so. Or stare without moving an eyelash. Or suck something and *become the sucking.*

53. Without support for feet or hands, sit only on buttocks. Suddenly, *the centering.*

54. In an easy position, gradually pervade an area between the armpits *into great peace.*

55. See *as if for the first time* a beauteous person or an ordinary object.

56. With mouth slightly open, keep mind in the middle of tongue. Or, as breath comes silently in, feel the sound *HH.*

57. When on a bed or a seat, let yourself become *weightless,* beyond mind.

58. In a moving vehicle, by rhythmically swaying, *experience*. Or in a still vehicle, by letting yourself swing in slowing invisible circles.

59. Simply by looking into the blue sky beyond clouds, *the serenity*.

60. Shakti, see all space as if already absorbed in your own head *in the brilliance*.

61. Waking, sleeping, dreaming, know you as *light*.

62. In rain during a black night, enter that *blackness* as the form of forms.

63. When a moonless raining night is not present, close eyes and find blackness before you. Opening eyes, *see blackness*. So faults disappear forever.

64. Just as you have the impulse to do something, *stop*.

65. Center on the sound *a-u-m* without any *a* or *m*.

66. Silently intone a word ending in *AH*. Then in the *HH* effortlessly, *the spontaneity*.

67. Feel yourself as *pervading* all directions, far, near.

68. Pierce some part of your nectar-filled form with a pin, and gently enter *the piercing*.

69. Feel: My thought, I-ness, internal organs—*me*.

70. Illusions deceive. Colors circumscribe. Even divisibles are *indivisible*.

71. When some desire comes, consider it. Then, suddenly, *quit it*.

72. Before desire and before knowing, how can I say I am? Consider. Dissolve in *the beauty*.

73. With your entire consciousness in the very start of desire, of knowing, *know*.

74. O Shakti, each particular perception is limited, disappearing *in omnipotence*.

75. In truth forms are inseparate. Inseparate are omnipresent being and your own form. Realize each as made of this *consciousness*.

76. In moods of extreme desire, be *undisturbed*.

77. This so-called universe appears as a juggling, a picture show. To be happy look upon it *so*.

78. O Beloved, put attention neither on pleasure or pain but *between these*.

79. Toss attachment for body aside, realizing *I am everywhere*. One who is everywhere is joyous.

80. Objects and desires exist in me as in others. So accepting, let them be *translated*.

81. The appreciation of objects and subjects is the same for an enlightened as for an unenlightened person. The former has one greatness: he remains *in the subjective mood*, not lost in things.

82. Feel the consciousness of each person as your own consciousness. So, leaving aside concern for self, *become each being*.

83. Thinking no thing, will limited-self *unlimit*.

84. Believe *omniscient, omnipotent, pervading*.

85. As waves come with water and flames with fire, so the universal waves *with us*.

86. Roam about until exhausted and then, dropping to the ground, in this dropping *be whole*.

87. Suppose you are gradually being deprived of strength or of knowledge. At the instant of deprivation, *transcend*.

88. Listen while the ultimate mystical teaching is imparted: Eyes still, without winking, at once become *absolutely free*.

89. Stopping ears by pressing and rectum by contracting, enter the *sound of sound*.

90. At the edge of a deep well look steadily into its depths until—*the wondrousness*.

91. Wherever your mind is wandering, internally or externally, at this very place, *this*.

92. When vividly aware through some particular sense, keep in *the awareness*.

93. At the start of sneezing, during fright, in anxiety, above a chasm, flying in battle, in extreme curiosity, at the beginning of hunger, at the end of hunger, be uninterruptedly *aware*.

94. Let attention be at a place where you are seeing some past happening, and even your form, having lost its present characteristics, *is transformed*.

95. Look upon some object, then slowly withdraw your sight from it, then slowly withdraw your thought from it. *Then.*

96. Devotion *frees.*

97. Feel an object before you. Feel the absence of all other objects but this one. Then, leaving aside the object-feeling and the absence-feeling, *realize.*

98. The purity of other teachings is as impurity to us. In reality know *nothing* as pure or impure.

99. This consciousness exists as each being, *and nothing else exists.*

100. Be the *unsame same* to friend as to stranger, in honor and dishonor.

101. When a mood against someone or for someone arises, do not place it on the person in question, but *remain centered.*

102. Suppose you contemplate something beyond perception, beyond grasping, beyond not being, *you.*

103. Enter space, *supportless, eternal, still.*

104. Wherever your attention alights, at this very point, *experience*.

105. Enter the sound of your name and, through this sound, *all sounds*.

106. I am existing. This is mine. This is this. O Beloved, even in such know *illimitably*.

107. This consciousness is the spirit of guidance of each one. *Be this one*.

108. Here is a sphere of change, change, change. Through change *consume change*.

109. As a hen mothers her chicks, mother particular knowings, particular doings, *in reality*.

110. Since, in truth, bondage and freedom are relative, these words are only for those terrified with the universe. This universe is a reflection of minds. As you see many suns in water *from one sun*, so see bondage and liberation.

111. Each thing is perceived through knowing. The self shines in space through knowing. *Perceive one being* as knower and known.

112. Beloved, at this moment let mind, knowing, breath, form, *be included*.

# What Is Zen?

TRY if you wish. But Zen comes of itself. True Zen shows in everyday living, CONSCIOUSNESS in action. More than any limited awareness, it opens every inner door to our infinite nature.

Instantly mind frees. How it frees! False Zen wracks brains as a fiction concoted by priests and salesmen to peddle their own wares.

Look at it this way, inside out and outside in: CONSCIOUSNESS everywhere, inclusive, through you. Then you can't help living humbly, in wonder.

"What is Zen?"

*One answer:* Inayat Khan tells a Hindu story of a fish who went to a queen fish and asked: "I have always heard about the sea, but what is this sea? Where is it?"

The queen fish explained: "You live, move, and have your being in the sea. The sea is within you and without you, and you are made of sea, and you will end in sea. The sea surrounds you as your own being."

*Another answer:*